THE ART OF DIVINATION

THE ROLE OF CONSCIOUSNESS AND WILL
IN STEPPING OUTSIDE TIME

WILLIAM DOUGLAS HORDEN

3 + 4 :: 6 + 1 :: RETURN

Delok Publishing, Ithaca

© 2020

ISBN: 9781670496751

DEDICATION

TAOIST MASTER BRUCE DAVID EICHELBERGER

TO DIVINE IS HUMAN

CONTENTS

PREFACE

Divination is an ancient art.

The diviners of antiquity were called priests and priestesses. They were held to be in contact with the spirit world. And they were considered worthy of their calling due to the self-purification and self-cultivation regimen they had made their lifelong practice.

The gods, in other words, trusted them to be honorable and entrusted them with their messages. The original diviners answered a high calling then and their spiritual descendants answer the same calling today, ever dedicated to being worthy of the trust—both human and divine—placed in them.

As the modern industrial mind relinquishes control of human destiny, the ancient spiritual mind will take up the reins and attempt to salvage civilization while returning it to a balanced harmony with nature.

The need for the path of foresight, wisdom, and empathy will increase—both for individuals and civilization as a whole—as difficult decisions multiply and new solutions are sought. Such a path is that provided by the oracular voice of the spirit world—the voice of the Oracle whose foresight, wisdom and empathy ring true in the depths of the human soul.

This is doubly so because of the loss of faith in institutional religions as they are increasingly perceived as relics of the modern industrial mind's contorted justifications for desecrating nature and human nature. As their inability to forgive and rejoin humanity as a whole isolates them more and more, individuals worldwide return to the universal belief in the sacredness of everything—a belief buoyed by each generation's growing sensitivity to the living spirit within every material form.

The inevitability of this return to a spiritual civilization is affirmed in the pronouncements of myriad divinations by diviners worldwide.

INTRODUCTION

From the perspective of divination, neither Consciousness nor Will—as we ordinarily think of them—play any role in the act of stepping outside time. It takes years of practice and self-cultivation, however, before diviners achieve such an uncontrived resonance with the Oracle.

Diviners, it has been said, are not born—they are created by a strange alchemy of shadow and light, the mysterious conjunction of the living relics of the eldest star and the ephemerality of morning dew. Products of improbable coincidences and otherworldly intuition, they come to the traditional methods of divination with raw skills, often honed over forgotten lifetimes, but still in need of the training to authentically transcend the sense of self so as to be in service to the One.

The practice outlined herein is dedicated to shortening the diviner's path to uncontrived resonance with the Oracle.

Spirit Speaks from Outside Time

The diviner's first-hand knowledge of the numinous presence of the sacred stands in sharp contrast to the modern industrial mind's tendency toward automatically reducing spiritual truths to innocuous clichéd abstractions. It is from this fundamental experience that the elder wisdom traditions have based practices that heighten our collective capacity to benefit the world of manifestation by accurately interpreting the intentions of the pre-manifestation world.

Many Methods, One Oracle

As there is One Spirit that speaks to us, there is only One Speaking, One Oracle. The root meaning of the word *oracle* is, after all, simply the Latin *orare*, meaning *to speak*. The Oracle, then, is the *Speaking* of the One Spirit, regardless of the specific divinatory method through which it speaks.

In that vein, this book is intended as a companion for diviners in their relationship with the Oracle, whether the method they are using to communicate with the Oracle is the I Ching, Astrology, Tarot, Tonalpohuolli, Geomancy,

Cabala, Numerology, Feng Shui, Runes, Crystal Gazing, or any of the other time-tested methods of divination.

To be a *diviner* means penetrating the veil of the five senses and perceiving the eternal at work in the temporal.

By way of an analogy: a water dowser, also called a *water diviner*, does not look for *future* water—on the contrary, the dowser is looking for *present* water that is hidden beneath the surface. So it is with the act of divination: we are not trying to tell the future; we are, on the contrary, attempting to know what is *present* beneath the surface of the five senses.

The *art of divination* is to step outside the flow of time in order to clearly perceive and accurately interpret the symbols of the eternal ideas. This act of perceiving the unfolding of present circumstances is an integral aspect of adapting to and guiding the ongoing manifestation of spirit.

It used to be that divinations were cast for the emperor to decide, for example, if the capital city ought to be moved or if the nation ought to go to war. Every divination ought to be undertaken with a similar sense of *gravitas*.

Divination is Magic

A person asks a question of *something invisible* in their surroundings; in response, they receive an answer that addresses their concerns directly.

To be absolutely clear: a person asks a question of *something invisible* and that something invisible hears them and answers in a way that is both comprehensible and meaningful. Furthermore, this is a repeatable event with extremely high degrees of congruence between questions and answers—and is a repeatable event spanning thousands of years and millions of querents.

Most to the point, this is a sequence of events that cannot occur in the absence of spirit. For this reason, it is called supernatural, or magic—a continuation of shamanic traditions rooted in animism, the most ancient religion held across the whole of the world in indigenous cultures. The worldview of those elder cultures asserts that everything is living spirit—that everything has a soul.

From such a perspective, there is little difference between spirit and soul: whereas spirit is universal, soul is an individuated facet of spirit that has developed an identity.

Since ancient times, the relationship between spirit and souls has been visualized as that between the ocean and its waves.

Diviners are Servants

The overall focus of this book is the breaking down of the barriers holding us back from communing directly with the Mind of the Oracle.

In other words, *it is the diviner's inner nature, and not their skill or knowledge, that allows them to hear and interpret Spirit's messages.*

In this context, *inner nature* refers to the individual's way of acting, feeling, thinking and being. As the ancient sage, Heraclitus, taught: *Character is Fate.* The One Spirit opens its heart to souls who sacrifice their own interests to those of the common good—its own inner nature resonates with that of selfless and benevolent individuals who place the needs and wellbeing of others above their own.

To genuinely be of service is to be led to one's destiny: character is fate. No preconceptions adequately prepare one for the degree of satisfaction and sense of fulfillment that comes from seeing another advance on their soul's path.

From this, one may correctly conclude that the present work is an attempt to outline *the emotional, mental and spiritual practice* of uncontrived resonance with the Oracle.

Though this small book aims to stand as a boon companion to any who *practice* divination, may it also serve as a worthy ally to all who *aspire* to the art.

Part One

The Role of Consciousness

CHAPTER 1

FOUNDATION

Consciousness is the sum of the body's experiences.

From the point of view of elder spiritual traditions, this means that consciousness is the acquired knowledge of the lower soul, in contrast to the eternal understanding that the higher soul carries with it across lifetimes.

By *acquired knowledge* is meant that the self-awareness possessed by an individual's consciousness is conditioned by the family, culture and historical era into which the individual is born. Even those individuals able to cast off all such influences remain nonetheless limited in their perceptions and sensitivities by the range of the five senses.

In other words, the self-awareness that consciousness gives rise to is a *conditioned self* whose experiential horizons are bounded by the linear nature of time, the physical laws of nature, and the sum of the body's experiences.

The *unconditioned self*, on the other hand, is a higher-order intelligence, or awareness, with no practical bounds on its potential participation in Creation. Also called the *true self*, or *original self*, it is the self-aware aspect of the higher soul, which is itself the self-identity of an individualized embodiment of the One Spirit.

Unbounded by time, space or the body, the true self provides the direct link in the communication between the Oracle and the diviner's awareness.

CHAPTER 2

IMAGE

Consciousness is both image and mirror.

There is a space between the sky and its reflection in the lake—a space that holds its place, despite alternatingly following the sky upward into unknown heights and following the lake downward into unknown depths.

Ascending into the heights, consciousness reveals its potential lucidity to itself. Descending into the depths, consciousness reveals its potential obscurity to itself. While these two are unquestionably one—the fruits and roots of a great living tree of experience—they could hardly be more different in action.

The lucid potential we can call *active consciousness*, while the obscure potential, *passive consciousness*.

When someone asks you, "What is one hundred and one plus ten?" and you reply, One hundred and eleven," you have just engaged active consciousness in order to respond to something in the present moment.

On the other hand, when you are driving along the highway and spontaneously recall some regret from years past, reliving the experience yet again for the thousandth time, which then triggers a cascade of memories of other past regrets, all of which sink you into a dark mood that you are all-too-familiar with, you have just engaged passive consciousness and its automatic generation of unbidden thoughts.

Active consciousness is intelligent, playful, adaptive, curious, and infinitely inventive. It is insightful thought, careful consideration, fruitful conclusions, discoveries and sound logic. It is capable of fine distinctions of meaning and nuanced interpretations.

Passive consciousness is the habit mind.

It is at this point that the diviner must engage in objective self-awareness by turning the light of active consciousness onto the obscurity of passive consciousness. Otherwise, the habit mind throws up insurmountable obstacles to authentic divination.

22

The obscure nature of passive consciousness lies in the fact that it is rooted in the physical organ of the brain. This rootedness within physicality creates a barrier to active consciousness, which is decidedly non-physical. This is similar to the fragrance of a flower, in the sense that the habit mind of passive consciousness is like the flower rooted in the soil and the active consciousness is like its fragrance, carried by the wind far and wide from its physical roots.

Active consciousness, then, is unable to *consciously* pursue its own arising from the physical organ of the brain. But because of the scientific awareness of modern active consciousness, we know that the roots of consciousness lie in the synaptic connections linking neurons in the brain—connections that hold, among other things, memories of past difficulties, especially the negative thoughts and emotions associated with traumas and shocks. These synaptic pathways link associated thoughts, emotions and memories in such a way that they are *reinforced* the more often they are relived as a conscious experience. And the more they are reinforced, the stronger *habits* they become.

But *why* do we keep reliving such negative experiences?

Not by choice, obviously. If not by choice, then, how are we *compelled* to constantly recall—and reexperience—past experiences? If not by choice, in other words, what mechanism triggers past associations in such a way as to automatically generate habitual unbidden thoughts?

The answer lies in the very physical roots of life itself. By which we mean, the genetic code. Again, it is the scientific awareness of active consciousness that permits us to know that DNA is not just the code of life, but the origin of the body's automatic functioning. What we know is that the goal of DNA is the reproduction of DNA. Its primary function is the survival of the physical body in order that it continues to make more DNA.

DNA, in other words, does not care about the happiness of the individual, or the satisfaction it has in its relationships or occupation. What it cares about is the individual surviving to make more DNA. This means that happiness, for example, is inconsequential, in that it might result in a relaxed individual so comfortable with its environment that it lets its guard down and falls prey to early death.

In animals and, therefore, in human beings, DNA has three principal mechanisms by which it assures a greater chance of survival: *anxiety, lust and dominance*.

Anxiety assures that the individual remains on alert, always paying attention to any threat, or *potential threat*. Lust assures that the individual is drawn to potential mates with which to procreate and contribute to the next generation of DNA. Dominance assures that the individual possesses certain characteristics, such as strength, intelligence, attractiveness, adaptability, etc., that heightens its chance of survival and passes those on to the next generation of DNA.

These three mechanisms are, from the point of view of DNA, absolutely essential to the survival of individual organisms, which in turn are essential to the reproduction of DNA.

Question of the First Magnitude: So how does DNA compel the individual human being to keep the focus of conscious attention on these three behaviors?

Answer of the First Magnitude: By secreting chemicals and hormones in the brain that trigger the personal associations of past experiences within the synaptic pathways.

In other words: To assure individual survival and DNA reproduction, DNA (which is in every cell of the body except red blood cells) instructs the brain to constantly secrete those chemicals and hormones that trigger (among other autonomic functions of the body) the mechanisms of anxiety, lust and dominance in the present moment.

These universal mechanisms trigger the individual's personal experiences, which have, through repeated reexperiencing, become habits of thought, emotion and memory. At this point, the universal becomes the individual: the unconscious physical mechanisms now break the surface of consciousness as past states and events are again relived as if occurring in the present moment.

Obviously, the conscious reliving of distressful events acts as a feedback to the brain, which perceives a new threat (anxiety), a potential release of sexual desire (lust), or a challenge to one's status (dominance)—the result of which is the release of more chemicals and hormones in the brain and an escalation in the range or intensity of associations carried by the synaptic pathways.

Passive consciousness is entirely mechanical.

The habit thoughts, emotions and memories carried by the neural pathways *do* reach consciousness but *not* because they are willed or intended. They arrive unbidden, intrusive and irrepressible. It is for this reason that this form of consciousness is called passive.

It is only when active consciousness turns its attention to the autonomic functioning of passive consciousness that the habit mind can be viewed as an *automatic functioning* of the body, independent of the thoughts *intentionally* called to mind by the true self. Without recognizing the difference between the artificial, conditioned, self arising from the lower soul's habit mind of passive consciousness, and the original, true, self manifesting from the higher soul's influence on active consciousness, diviners remain unable to perform their duty as a clear-hearted conduit of the Oracle's message.

The higher soul's allotment of celestial understanding allows active consciousness to train its passive counterpart to *revert to stillness*. Simply stated, *there is no other single act more essential to the art of divination than this practice of quieting the habit mind in order to hear Oracle's whisper.*

27

In the most practical sense, a person's self-defeating thoughts, feelings and behaviors are the result of placing their intent on the wrong image-symbols. As a remedy, divination replaces those with transformative, self-creating image-symbols upon which the querent may concentrate long afterward.

CHAPTER 3

MIRROR

Consciousness is both mirror and image.

Active consciousness is able to train passive consciousness because they are both rooted in the same synaptic pathways of the physical brain.

Whereas passive consciousness compulsively relives past events, active consciousness utilizes the neural pathways to secure a firm foundation of cogent associations, accurate memory and creative leaps of inductive reasoning. Active consciousness differs from passive consciousness in that it does not automatically view new experiences as potential threats, other people as potential mates, nor relationships as battlefields of status.

Elder spiritual traditions long ago recognized the need to bring the artificial self of passive consciousness under control in order to allow active consciousness to establish a relationship with the higher soul and manifest the true self within the present lifetime.

For example, there is the story of a youth who approached a great teacher, asking if he could be taken on as his disciple. *Of course, of course,* replied the teacher, *but first, go home and kill your parents.*

This phrase, *kill your parents,* was the teacher's way of symbolically pointing to the accumulation of a lifetime of conditioned knowledge that begins with parental tutelage. While the phrase may sound overly harsh to modern sensibilities, it reflects the seriousness of purpose with which the practitioner undertakes the pacification of the habit mind. It is also a brilliant way to point to the *intimacy* of the habit mind—how we cherish it, even as we resent its hold over us. To silence the habit mind feels like the death of that which has been closest to us our whole life: a sense of self, a *me*, an *I*, utterly determined by the accident of birth to family, culture and historical era.

For this reason, other traditions called it the Great Death, pointing to the necessity of sacrificing the artificial self of the ego-identity in order to experience the Celestial Ego.

The advances in knowledge by active consciousness allow us to understand the mechanisms underlying the problems that elder traditions recognized so clearly and the solutions to which they devised so concrete methods. Universally, the ancients addressed the barriers to spiritual communion with concrete practices calling for the embodiment of a higher-level awareness.

People differ only in their sensitivity to the One.

Everyone hopes to hear the voice of Spirit clearly and to live their lives according to its messages. Not everyone, however, has the good fortune to have access to teachings or traditions that treat training the habit mind in a coherent, disciplined and spiritually sound manner. Likewise, not everyone has the temperament to consistently, sincerely and rigorously put such teachings into practice.

Diviners, though, do not have the luxury of ignorance nor indolence in this matter. The clarity of their perceptions and interpretations depends on the degree to which they can hear the Oracle's messages without any distortion caused by intrusive personal associations.

It is the body that must awaken.

Music soars free of the instrument that produces it. It enters the awareness of others, impacting them in rewarding ways. It interacts with the music produced by other instruments, the synergistic effect impacting performers and audience in rewarding ways.

But—if the instrument is not properly tuned, then the entire expression and interpretation of the song is ruined from the outset.

Likewise, if the passive consciousness of the physical brain is not tuned by active consciousness, then the entire expression and interpretation of the Oracle is ruined from the outset.

It is similar to music soaring free from a radio. If the radio is not tuned properly to the station, then the music is ruined by the static. It is necessary to properly tune the *medium* of the music, the physical radio, the conduit of the music, to the invisible station carrying the music to all—only then is the static eliminated and the music heard clear and pure.

How, then, do we tune passive consciousness?

Let us return to what we know about the habit mind and, in particular, how habits are formed and extinguished. Habits are formed by repeated response to previous mental experience; they are reinforced by some reward that satisfies an unconscious need. *Habits are extinguished by removing the reward.*

In the case of passive consciousness and its formation of the habit mind, the *unconscious need* is to relieve the tension produced by DNA in triggering a past thought, emotion or memory. The *reinforcement* is the act of reliving the thought, emotion or memory. And the *reward* is the heightened intensity of discomfort produced by the triggered tension—for it is this discomfort and tension that fulfill DNA's demand for heightened vigilance. The irony, of course, is that this is a reward only for DNA, and in no way one of contentment or wellbeing for the individual.

In order to extinguish the habitual responses of passive consciousness it is necessary to remove the reward—which is to say, to *cease reinforcing, or reliving, the habitual thoughts, emotions, and memories.*

This brings us to one of the great insights of the elder traditions, which provides us with the mechanism for tuning passive consciousness to active consciousness, and can be paraphrased thus:

You can have only one conscious thought at a time.

It does not matter how fast thoughts fly, the gate through which they must pass into consciousness permits but one to cross its threshold at a time.

The practice itself follows from these now-evident rules —

1. Cease reinforcing habit mind by no longer reliving unbidden thoughts, emotions and memories, and
2. Control the one thought entering consciousness at a time

The ancients understood these mechanisms and developed various means of utilizing them to pacify the habit mind, opening consciousness to higher-order awareness. Most obvious and well-known of such mechanisms are *mantras* and *koans*, which students were given with explicit instructions to *repeat constantly, holding them in mind at all times*.

From our current perspective, we can see the functional rationale for these practices devised by the ancients in order to *convert passive consciousness into active consciousness*.

By training students to hold a single sound, word or phrase in their conscious awareness *all the time*, students learned to block passive consciousness from arising (since the one conscious thought at a time was already occupied) and expand active consciousness to thus occupy every waking moment (since they were constantly repeating the mantra or koan every waking moment).

Other traditional practices include meditation, where students are trained to simply bring their active consciousness onto the habit thoughts that arise in their meditation and then transfer that exercise of mindfulness to every waking moment outside of meditation, as well.

The ignorant and indolent mind will argue that it is too difficult to maintain constant attention to its thinking, without stopping to consider that it is already talking to itself in the form of habit thoughts every waking moment of passive consciousness. It is just instead of being dragged across·the field by the horse, this practice allows one to be carried by the noble steed of blood and bone toward the consciously chosen destination of spiritual freedom, spontaneity and creativity.

The most immediate and easiest to describe variation of the practice can be visualized as training a watchdog who is repeatedly and consistently barking at birds flying high overhead. Of course, you step outside and call out *No!* or *Enough!* in a firm tone of voice.

Here, we convert passive consciousness into active consciousness by creating a new habit, consciously repeating the word *No!* or *Enough!* every waking moment when not already engaged in active consciousness.

This has the effect, of course, of blocking habit thoughts before they get started, assuring that we do not reinforce them by reliving them yet again. Lacking reinforcement over a long enough period of time, the compulsive, reflexive nature of the habit thoughts is extinguished and they no longer arise unbidden. Those who take up the *No!* or *Enough!* as a mantra or koan upon which the mind is to focus all the time find that the internal dialog of the habit mind diminishes until one day, active consciousness stands alone in a tranquil space of open presence, where the voice of the true self rings unmistakably clear and true.

It is at this point that one stops the practice.

It is essential to keep in mind that the entire aim of the practice is to *enliven* awareness, not deaden it. It is, in fact, the habit mind of passive consciousness that deadens awareness, creating a trance-like state all too similar to sleepwalking through life. By eradicating this deadening pressure on awareness, we enliven active consciousness to fulfill its potential of occupying the open space of the present moment of awareness.

We are eliminating the static, in other words, not the music.

In this sense, the result of the practice is very different than the practice. Once the habit mind has been pacified, we hear the new habit of our mantra-koan still repeating in the background of awareness — only now, the *No!* directive has transformed into *Know......*and the *Enough!* proscription has changed into a heartfelt recognition that one now *is enough, has enough, will be enough.*

With this review of the nature of consciousness and its transmutation, we are prepared to advance toward our goal of experiencing and interpreting the Oracle in accord with its intent.

CHAPTER 4

HEAVEN AND EARTH

Divinatory space is where Heaven and Earth unite.

THE ONENESS OF TIME

THE REALM OF THE ORACLE

THE MIND OF HEAVEN

THE TIMELESS

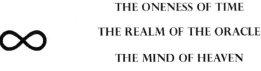

DIVINATORY SPACE

It can be visualized as a vast, immeasurable space of pure Awareness, a horizontal plane running from beginningless origin to endless destination. From this horizontal plane of timeless eternity there hang, like so many icicles, or stalactites, the infinite number of linear moments of time running from past to future. Though ephemeral to consciousness as it passes through them, each moment of time is, in fact, as eternal as the timeless eternity it manifests—frozen forever in their perfect ephemerality, the moments of time stand like indestructible landmarks of the unfolding of Creation from beginningless origin to endless destination.

From the diagram above, we can see that the boundless horizontal plane is identified by several names: the Oneness of Time, the Realm of the Oracle, the Mind of Heaven, the Timeless. Other names for it are the One Spirit, the Spirit World, the Imaginal, the Nagual, the Bardo, the Dreamtime, the World Soul, the One Mind.

It is the role of the diviner to unite Heaven and Earth.

This is to say, that the diviner establishes the connection between the timeless horizontal plane of spirit and the timebound vertical moment of time in the plane of life.

We can visualize this union as a lightning bolt that connects one charged pole in the sky with another on the ground. The resulting coupling produces a powerful discharge of energy, heat and light that illuminates the whole of the landscape.

In this sense, the sky is the spiritual potential of the timeless awareness of the Oracle. The charged pole in the sky represents the diviner's relationship with the Oracle, while the charged pole on the ground represents the question, or issue at hand, that is being addressed to the Oracle. The ground itself, of course, represents the entirety of linear time and, in particular, the specific moment of time in which the divination occurs. The lightning bolt represents the divination itself, meaning the Oracle's answer and the diviners' interpretation together. Its energy breaks up stagnation, enlivening intention. Its heat brings warmth to the cold of confusion, pain and loneliness. And, its light shatters the dark, illuminating understanding.

To reiterate: *The charged pole in the sky represents the diviner's relationship with the Oracle.* The ancients held that the Spirit of Nature recognizes and nurtures every being in Nature, just as the World Soul recognizes and nurtures every soul within it. Diviners have a unique relationship with the eternal awareness of the One Spirit based on their mystical union with *The Unchanging* at the heart of the individual and the universal — at the heart of the microcosm and the macrocosm. This mystical union is the fusion of essence-to-essence that both voids consciousness (in the sense of self-awareness separate from the experience) even as it transmutes it into the transcendental awareness of the underlying perfection of all things. This underlying perfection of all things points directly to the inevitable mystical reunion of all things, which marks the return of all things to *The One* — the state also called *The Oneness of All Things*. The diviner's experience of this state has long been described symbolically as the drop of water returning to the ocean.

This is to say that the timeless, oceanic awareness of the One Mind (of which the Oracle is the form of expression open to communication with human nature) is accessible to those with the sensitivity and perseverance to step outside the *world of change* and enter *The Unchanging*. In the diagram above, the world of change is represented by the accumulation of all the vertical moments of time and the Unchanging is represented by the horizontal plane of the Timeless.

Returning to our visualization of the lightning bolt, it is instructive to consider the two charged poles together: *The charged pole in the sky represents the diviner's relationship with the Oracle, while the charged pole on the ground represents the question, or issue at hand, that is being addressed to the Oracle.* Regardless of whether the question is the diviner's or another's, it is the diviner who carries it to the Oracle—just as the diviner's relationship with the Oracle is established by the diviner's unstinting devotion to the divine nature of the One Spirit.

Treating the questioning as sacred, treating the answering as sacred—the diviner fuses Heaven and Earth, joining the mundane and the divine in a singular burst of spiritual illumination. The One Spirit speaks through the Oracle, which already has a long-standing relationship with human beings based on a fixed number of symbols—the traditional meanings of which the diviner devotes a lifetime of study—and it is in the ancient language of these symbols that the Oracle breaks into the timebound world of change with its message for the living. Here, it is the diviner's intimacy with the Oracle's symbols that translates the timeless, universal message into a language appropriate to the individual situation, culture and historical era.

The impact of the divination can be shattering, disrupting illusion and preconception as the uniting of Heaven and Earth should. Speaking from the wider context of universal awareness and infinite lifetimes, the Oracle's reply to the matter-at-hand illuminates its underlying essence and purpose in the life path of the questioner. Its lessons, couched in symbols of the eternal balancing between Light and Dark, clarify the difference between those choices leading to disappointment and those leading to fulfillment.

It is with the diviner's interpretive skills that the Oracle's symbolic speech renders the rupturing of illusions and preconceptions into the revealing of new insights and genuine freedom. Since ancient times, the Oracle's gift to human nature is the ability to see through illusion and achieve the spontaneity of action that gives birth to the creative life.

CHAPTER 5

THE ORACLE

Divination does not occur in a vacuum. It is the result of the need to see beneath the surface of appearances in order to grasp the underlying lines of development and discern the pitfalls and opportunities they hold. These words *pitfalls* and *opportunities* mean something different, of course, depending on the context of the divination.

For the diviner's part, every act of divination is a sacred ritual, an act of communion with spirit, nature and human nature.

Diviners consult the Oracle for one of five purposes:

1. For the diviner's own illumination
2. For the illumination of another individual
3. For the illumination of individuals in a relationship
4. For the illumination of a group, organization, or alliance
5. For the illumination of the public

Although people sometimes seek divinations with a single question or issue in mind, it is almost always the case that the question they have arrived at consciously is not the one the deeper aspects of themselves care most about. They are surprised, then, when the Oracle replies to the *unasked* question, the *unvoiced* concern, forgetting for the moment that the Oracle is responding to their entire Being, and not just the words they speak. As the manifestation of the One Mind closest to human nature, the Oracle is aware of all an individual's thoughts and concerns. As the manifestation of the One Spirit closest to human nature, the Oracle is aware of the entire span of an individual's past, present and future.

In light of this, the diviner may prefer to interview the querent informally, but thoroughly, touching on all facets of the person's life, giving them time to feel comfortable enough to free-associate across the entire span of their lifetime. Here, the diviner's heightened sense of *listening* to the Oracle is turned upon the querent, attending closely to both what is spoken and unspoken. Similarly, the diviner's heightened rapport with the symbolic speech of the Oracle is turned upon the querent, attending closely to the multiple meanings held by words and gestures. Given the comfort of the querent, the diviner may wish to ask clarifying questions occasionally in order to allow the other to bring forth everything held in mind and heart.

It can be useful for the diviner to keep in mind that *everyone speaks their own language*. This is to say, they use words to express what they have become accustomed to associate with them, a process deeply embedded in their own personal history. For this reason, the diviner may try to consciously avoid assuming that the querent's language is the same as the diviner's language—the querent's associations to words are what constitutes their own individual language, which makes the diviner's rapport with the querent important not just in listening and understanding the other, but in speaking and interpreting the Oracle's reply.

With a cloud of issues brought out into the open, the querent is not so surprised when the Oracle answers the unasked question—and the diviner is better aware of all issues at hand, and so abler to interpret the symbols of the Oracle's answer in their proper light.

Even with all this care, the Oracle may reply with a message that does not seem to apply at all to the querent. Diviners may consider in such circumstances that it is best to report the entire reading, anyway, since it is often the case that it is just those seemingly unrelated aspects of the divination that unexpectedly unlock the bound-up energy holding a person back from experiencing the most fulfilling life.

People hope for a transformative experience.

Although oftentimes an underlying unconscious desire, the real reason people engage in the ritual act of divination is the deep-seated wish to encounter the *numinous* and undergo thereby an empowering transformation of self. That such an encounter often turns on a revelatory moment, a spontaneous insight that places the puzzle pieces of their life into a suddenly more understandable and meaningful picture, means that the diviner must not fall into too literal and mundane interpretations of the Oracle's message.

People have become accustomed to "what is on the menu," in the sense of what they can expect in any given situation. What excites them, all the way down to the fascinated core curiosity of infancy, is to encounter "what is *not* on the menu." Conscientious diviners seek to establish an atmosphere and demeanor that do nothing to interfere with the querent's heightened expectation of the living potential within the divinatory space itself as well as within their own capacity to metamorphose.

People seek unconsciously to evolve, to better their intentions and emotions and responses to things—but given the limited perspective and ulterior motives of human beings, they do not trust themselves or others to provide the map to such changes. The traditional divinatory systems, however, they *can* trust, because they are repositories of accumulated wisdom, spanning thousands of years and hundreds of generations of wise and caring savants, that carry universal truths aimed at just such personal transformation. It follows that the most conscientious diviners are those who—

1. Create a sacred space conducive to heightened awareness
2. Empty consciousness of attachment to the outcome of the divination
3. Do nothing to hold the querent back from realizing the fullest possible meaning of the Oracle's message

These three steps make up the core activity of the diviner. Other forms of participation, such as listening to the querent closely or interpreting the Oracle's symbols elegantly, are essential, as well, but they are the visible flesh of the divination that depend on these three steps comprising the invisible bones, so to speak, of the reading.

Divinations are healings.

Transformational experiences are, by nature, healing. They resolve distress by *untying knots* and *pulling out nails*—by breaking up the stagnation within consciousness that is blocking a joyful and fulfilling life. Healing experiences restore a person's capacity for joyousness by revealing new and unexpected resources—within and without—by which a new and more dynamic equilibrium can be lived. They are cathartic, inasmuch as they release the pent up energies trapped in distressful emotions, memories or sensations. From this perspective, it is equally valid to say that healing experiences are, by nature, transformational.

It is instructive to consider the traditional use of divination in indigenous cultures for healing rituals, wherein the diviner seeks to find the hidden cause of a person's distress. In order to discover what is hidden from the senses, such divinations use an array of methods, including: corn kernels; crystals and special stones; plant medicine; and, egg yolks. By such means, the Oracle reveals not just the cause of distress but also the means of "cleansing" or "purifying" the soul, thus relieving it of further unease.

It is no different with other, more familiar divinatory systems, such as Astrology, Tarot, I Ching, etc., whereby the Oracle's symbols illuminate the hidden cause of the soul's distress and, in doing so, transform its very nature in a spontaneous act of restoring wholeness. This is intrinsic to the ancient practice of "cleansing" and "purification," which recognizes the original perfection of the soul and understands that its wholeness depends not on adding anything to it but, rather, on eliminating the offending element originating from the outside. In this sense, it resembles polishing, or cleansing, the surface of a mirror of dust from elsewhere; or, of purifying water of contaminants extrinsic to its nature.

The diviner's role in all this resembles walking a tightrope between Heaven and Earth. Like their spiritual ancestors, the *spirit mediums* of old, diviners balance between the spirit world and the human world, careful to fall into neither even as they unite them within the microcosm of their own awareness. Querents come to a divination with concerns from both the spirit and human realms; they seek to find their way upon both the eternal path of their soul and the timebound path of their day-to-day life.

For this reason, diviners must weave these two threads into a coherent *narrative*, diligently avoiding over-emphasizing either the spiritual or the material, either the mystical or the rational, either the eternal or the transitory, either the sacred or the mundane. The divination's narrative emerges from the Oracle's timeless symbols responding to the querent's timebound circumstances, providing them with both a wider context and a narrower focus of direction and momentum.

Marshaling the Oracle's symbols into a lucid narrative accurately reflecting Spirit's message—this is the diviner's sacred responsibility to the querent and the Oracle, both.

CHAPTER 6

THE SOUL

Divine Fire is the lightning bolt uniting Eternity and Life.

How does one speak about the soul without speaking about immortality? How does one speak about immortality without speaking about eternity? How does one speak about eternity without speaking about the immortal being dwelling within it?

This is a matter of utmost importance to diviners because they literally swim in the ocean of soul. All Creation is a text of symbols that reveals the Mind of Heaven. The *objective space* in which all its images occur is *psyche,* or *soul.* Consider for a moment the dream experience: the *dream space* in which the dream occurs is nothing but *psyche.* Everything in that space is comprised of the same substance, *psyche.* This *psychic substance* makes up the whole of the dream and, indeed, the whole of the world, since awareness is conscious of nothing outside it.

It is for this reason that some elder traditions point to one's life and say that it ought to be understood to be a dream. This is because ordinary waking awareness is always to some extent experiencing the world through this primary sense organ—the *imaginal soul*. Deeper and prior to the conscious and unconscious minds, this most profound imagination perceives living *psychic substance* instead of the "dead matter" of the visible universe as interpreted by the modern industrial consciousness.

Closer to the unconscious than the conscious mind, the imaginal soul experiences life as the psychic substance of a dream space, its infinite elements in a constant state of flux and transformation into one another. Covered over by the conscious mind and barely uncovered by the unconscious mind *except during dreams*, the psychic substance of the soul viscerally experiences the wildness of symbolic and emotional forces emanated by the images it encounters.

Though most people pass their entire lives with few of these perceptions reaching consciousness, they nonetheless make up a large portion of the diviner's experiences. Trained to see beneath the surface of appearances, diviners find the constantly transforming reality of the underlying harmony a world of pre-manifestation that both antedates and gives rise to the manifest world of appearances.

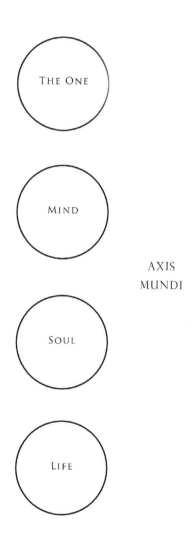

CLASSICAL VIEW OF THE EMANATIONS OF CREATION

The three lower spheres of the diagram above represent the emanations, or *Rays of Creation*, radiating from the original unity of The One. Each may be thought of as a denser materialization of The One than the emanation above it.

THE ONE: Transcendent *Being*. Ineffable. Unconditioned. Beyond rational concepts. Timeless. The Numinous. Oceanic Awareness. The Sphere of Universal Communion.

Mind: Realm of Pure Idea. Eternal Ideas, Archetypes. Number. *Nous*. Divine Intelligence. Realm of Understanding. Meaning. On the macrocosmic level: One Mind. On the microcosmic level: the individual mind.

Soul: Realm of *Psyche*, of Living Images. The Imaginal, Dreamtime, the *Nagual*. Realm of Intent. The In-Between World. The Bardo. On the macrocosmic level: the World Soul. On the microcosmic level: the individual soul.

Life: Realm of Nature. Realm of physical manifestation, of incarnation, of the material world. The *Tonal*. Realm of Memory. On the macrocosmic level: the universe, the world, the one body. On the microcosmic level: the individual body.

Transcendent Being gives rise to Pure Ideas, which give rise to Living Images, which give rise to Material Forms.

The elder spiritual traditions considered it self-evident that there exist two souls — the Celestial Soul and the Earthly Soul. The *higher soul* and the *lower soul*. As individuated embodiments of The One, the two souls are *able to move between the spheres of emanation*.

This last point cannot be over-emphasized, for it makes explicit the souls' capacity to ascend and descend the *Axis Mundi*, the World Axis. And it makes explicit the diviner's capacity to gain entry to the knowledge, meaning and wisdom within the different spheres of the World Axis.

From the perspective of this philosophy, the higher soul descends into the sphere of Life when a new infant is born and at that time invests that body with a spark of the Divine Fire that it carries in its womb. This spark ignites within the growing person and becomes the lower soul, which is conceived of as the individual repository of the lifetime. It consists of everything experienced by the imaginal soul, the unconscious mind and the conscious mind.

The lower soul, then, is the Memory of mortal existence, while the higher soul is the Understanding that comes from immortal existence.

The spark of Divine Fire within the lower soul grows stronger if nurtured properly, which involves in large part reducing the influence of passive consciousness and increasing the influence of active consciousness. It acts as an inner compass, guiding the lower soul to its reunion with the higher soul. This uniting of the lower and higher souls is termed a *yoga*, meaning a *yoking* of body and spirit, embodying the individual uniting of Heaven and Earth.

This union of higher and lower souls is intended to occur during the person's lifetime, so that upon the death of the body, the lower soul returns with the higher soul to The One, to the Sphere of Universal Communion. Should this yoking not occur during the person's lifetime, then the lower soul wanders lost and confused in the In-Between World: as Memory of the mortal lifetime, but lacking the Understanding of immortality, the lower soul constantly relives the lifetime unaware that the body has fallen away. It requires an intervention along the lines of the traditional soul retrieval to awaken such a lower soul so that it might finally reunite with the higher soul.

The *yoking* of the lower and higher souls is the spiritual counterpart to the DNA-generated commands to the physical body's autonomous functioning—it is a kind of *spiritual instinct*, analogous to the salmon's homing instinct to return to its spawning grounds, a universal need that individuals experience with widely-differing degrees of sensitivity.

The view of an earthly soul and a celestial soul helps orient diviners, affording them a perspective on the Oracle's message by revealing the divinatory space to be the *site of yoking* of the higher and lower souls. Because the Oracle's symbols are a repository of the wisdom and understanding of the higher souls of many generations of savants, its *speaking* calls out to the querent's lower soul in a long-remembered voice of *the other half*.

As to the reason for the lower soul's existence, animists hold a worldview wherein the Divine Fire is the universal element of generative energy coursing throughout the whole of Creation—and its incarnation within the Life Realm reveals to Transcendent Being an awareness of mortality by means of the direct experience of a mortal being: because it is the Memory of all the mortal body's experiences, once the lower soul yokes with the higher soul it is able to return together to *The One*.

Chapter 7

The Diviner

The soul divines itself.

Neither knowledge nor charisma alone are enough to draw one close to the Oracle. The lower soul, as it emerges from the practice of eliminating the passive consciousness and cultivating the subtler aspects of the active consciousness, turns a more objective eye on its character and the traits it has taken on.

Of particular note is one's *inclination*. This is meant in the sense of a *leaning into the next moment*. A person's inclination is developed relatively soon and sets in as a kind of Life Mood. Everyone knows what a mood is and how they feel when they come and go from day to day, moment by moment. But few are aware of the relatively stable and consistent mood they exude over the course of years. Of course, it is easy to say that is someone's disposition, their state of mind, that expresses their personality—but that does not speak to the issue of why that person does not change their Life Mood as easily as they change their daily or momentary moods. So effected are they by their Life Mood, that they are *already inclined* to exude it every moment of life—and the more temporary, fleeting moods are simply interruptions in their Life Mood.

Let us take for example, the need for attention. It is the emotional underpinning of the need that establishes the Life Mood. As immature as this need is, and as early on in life it makes itself felt, it lasts all the way through a lifetime for many people.

The lower soul evolves and observes and questions and acts. It outgrows the need and observes that it continues the inclination and questions why it does so when so many other people do not and it acts on this practice of self-divination by changing—such a transformation does not replace one Life Mood with another but, rather, frees up the soul to experience one mood after the other as spontaneous responses to inner and outer events. The act of simply noticing one's Life Mood and recognizing how stagnant it makes one's experiences feel is often enough to end it.

The soul divines itself. It evolves and observes and questions and acts. Everyone has different characteristics that require refining and it is the soul's responsibility to open up the individual's heart-mind to the life-affirming and self-constructive characteristics that bring human nature into accord with the One Spirit.

Humility. How can one stand before the stars or the grasses or the birds and not be blinded by the underlying perfection of All Creation? How can one stand before All Creation and not recognize the immensity of the Creative Forces that have wrought it? The soul extricates itself from feelings of self-importance and in doing so discovers its self-worth.

Sincerity. There is no greater tragedy in life than arriving at someone else's destination. Being true to one's path: to feel as one acts, to think as one feels, to speak as one thinks, to be as one speaks—leaving the road and stepping into the wilderness to find one's own way, such is one's true destination.

Reverence. Awakened to the sacredness of everything, one awakens to one's own sacred nature. Recognizing the divine nature of all things, one is faced with the most basic authentic question: *How does a sacred being treat all other sacred beings?* The answer to this question forms the foundation of the diviner's personal ethics. To live the reverential life is to live in awe of the underlying perfection of All Creation—and particularly of the incarnated spirit manifesting within all Nature.

Empathy. The basis of deep empathy is the recognition of shared mortality: every person lives knowing they are going to die—this extraordinary situation forces the diviner to recognize the courage and nobility of every human being and to extend to each the utmost respect and compassion for persevering in life despite the inevitability of death. This sense of empathy extends too, to every living being, like the animals, that share the pain of bodily harm and the fear of survival; and to those, too, like the trees and other plants, that live dependent on human nature for a shared existence of balance and harmony. The ability to put oneself in the place of another is essential to the diviner's ability to conduct beneficial divinations.

Generosity of Spirit. A giving and loving nature wishes others well. There is no place in such a soul for envy, jealousy, selfishness or a sense of lack—the wise and loving soul desires nothing but the prospering of every individual. As one great-souled being expressed it: *Without me changing in any way, I wish to be the lowliest of beings in All Creation.* Herein we have all five attributes shining forth: humility, sincerity, reverence, empathy and generosity of spirit. Herein is a soul so full of the underlying perfection of Creation that nothing further is necessary—except the wish that all other beings prosper even more so. Those who truly live the *ecstatic life* wish for all others to suffer even less than they do.

These are the light-bearing characteristics of the diviner's soul, to be certain. They are required because so much of the diviner's existence is spent in the Shadow of the Great Mystery and the inner light they cast keeps the dark of ill will and fear at bay.

Ascending the World Axis to enter the Realm of Psyche, the World Soul, diviners find their way by means of the imaginal soul. This is, at first, a singularly strange world of images constantly in flux as they transform into one another. Compared to the manifestation Realm of Life, this is a world marked by chaotification—rather than the order of differentiated bodies in time and space, the World Soul is similar to dream space in the sense that its elements exist in a realm of nondifferentiation. It is the pre-manifestation realm of psychic substance whose images take form in the realm of manifestation. With experience, diviners find their orientation in the Spirit World, the Nagual, the Dreamtime: their own imaginal soul attunes to The Imaginal Realm and the constant flux of images grows less chaotic as the diviners' understanding, perception and intent becomes more like that of a lucid dream.

This shift into not only *being-in* but also *participating-in* the World Soul is a determining factor in diviners' ability to work with the very mechanism of change itself.

To see pre-manifestation is to see coming manifestation.

In conducting a divination, diviners ascend the Axis Mundi in order to enter the World Soul and engage its symbols of coming manifestation in regards to the querent's concerns.

Before things take form in the manifestation realm, they exist as *images of psyche* in the pre-manifestation realm. As in dreams, these *images* appear as *symbols* with multiple dimensions of meaning and emotional significance. The diviner's capacity to enter the World Soul *as a soul* allows for a direct encounter, *soul-to-soul*, with these *symbols-of-things-to-come*. This is similar to the nondifferentiation state of dreams, where the absence of boundaries between dreamer and symbol results in a spontaneous communion, so that an immediate sharing of intention-emotion occurs: it is why the symbol appears to respond to the dreamer's emotion and the dreamer appears to know the intention of the symbol.

It is also why the *image-symbols* of the World Soul are called *angels*, the original meaning of which was not just *messenger*, but *harbinger*—which is why some dreams prove to be prophetic.

For diviners, this aspect of the practice begins by working with dreams:

1. Recognizing that the dream space is made entirely of psychic substance that (a) makes up the entirety of experience at the moment, and (b) morphs at will into different environments occupied by different image-symbols able to morph at will into one another.

2. Recognizing that the image-symbols are actually souls dwelling in the World Soul and one's dream is actually a tunnel, or passage, into the World Soul.

3. Recognizing that the image-symbols are not necessarily the true appearance of their souls.

4. Recognizing that one's own appearance in the dream space is as an image-symbol and not necessarily the true appearance of one's soul.

5. Recognizing that the image-symbols in the dream are reacting to one's own image-symbol.

6. Recognizing that the entirety of the psychic substance of the dream space is reacting to one's own image-symbol.

7. Recognizing that one's own image-symbol is either (a) an unconscious expression of one's Life Mood, or else (b) a conscious expression of one's intent.

It is the conscientious implementation of this dream work that attunes the diviner's imaginal soul to the World Soul, granting the diviner conscious entry into the realm of pre-manifestation. This allows diviners to perceive the image-symbols of the Oracle *as souls* and to discern the *timing* of their manifestation in the Life Realm.

This issue of timing is crucial to the act of divination, since the querent is often concerned not just with the possibility of some change manifesting but the possible timing of that manifestation, as well. It can be difficult to describe to others the limitations of such perceptions, however. That an image-symbol in the pre-manifestation realm is *ripening* in preparation to enter the manifestation realm points to the *developmental* aspect of change: it is possible to predict that Spring will arrive, but it is impossible to predict precisely when the weather will change in a particular region.

The reason for the lack of precision in the *if and when of change* in a divination is based on the image-symbol's dependence on *intent*. The soul of the image-symbol itself has an intent that expresses itself in two different ways. The first is the *content* of the intent, such as, *To benefit all at the same time*. The second is registered in terms of impetus: *magnitude and intensity*. The greater magnitude of intent, the greater possibility of manifestation. The same is true of intensity — the greater the intensity of intent, the greater the possibility of manifestation.

This is where the diviner's *participation* within the World Soul makes itself felt. For even though the magnitude and intensity of a single soul's intent can propel an image-symbol into manifestation, it is more generally the case that magnitude and intensity refer to the collective intent of a collaborative effort by an alliance of like-minded souls. It is for this reason that diviners spend time *dreaming* awake, exploring the Imaginal Realm of Dreamtime and entering into spiritual alliances with other souls whose intent expresses a content in harmony with their own.

From this perspective, the general principle is: The greater the number of souls concentrating on the manifestation of an image-symbol, the greater the *magnitude* of intent; the greater the passion focused on the manifestation of an image-symbol, the greater the *intensity* of intent. From this, the astute diviner recognizes how it is sometimes possible to assist in the manifestation of a querent's true needs.

As an example, let us suppose the overwhelming majority of people in the world decided they most wanted to live in a state of harmony and balance with one another, nature and spirit. Looking for an image-symbol upon which they could apply their intent, they chose something like *Return To*

Paradise, because it turned out that every culture had some vision of a previous age of an ideal world. The *content* of the image-symbol, then, would be *Return To Paradise*. The *magnitude* would be determined by the overwhelming number of souls focused on the image-symbol, and the *intensity* would be expressed by the degree of passionate heartfelt longing for its manifestation.

From this, it can be concluded that it is no simple matter for a diviner to judge these factors with anything but the loosest sense of approximation and the deepest sense of humility. This is particularly so because the content, magnitude and intensity of an image-symbol within the World Soul can be so intoxicating that it overwhelms the diviner's judgement, as in the case of an encounter with the image of *Paradise*.

Everything that takes form in manifestation has a soul.

This basic tenet of *animism* accounts for the diviner's innate communion with the entirety of the Realm of Life. Often referred to as *nature mysticism*, it is a relationship first and foremost of *body-to-body* communion, a deep-seated sense of the unity of all life, as if every individual thing were a node in an immense spider web of living beings.

But what is meant by *living beings* is different than what the modern industrial mind conceives. For, stone, too. is a living being—it breaks down to soil and is assimilated by the peach tree and converted ultimately to fruit and thence to consciousness when consumed by a person. It is the same with water and rain and so, with clouds and wind and open sky. And furthermore, with words themselves, which are the most direct and elegant manifestations of image-symbols taking form.

Secondarily, although perhaps more consciously, *nature mysticism* involves a *soul-to-soul* communion, as if every form radiates a formless and invisible light reflecting one's own. The soul of each body, whether person, animal, plant or mineral, shines forth as a palpable ripple of emotion and intent that one experiences with various degrees of accord, or resonance. The upshot, however, of *nature mysticism* is the diviner's complete and utter love of life, expressed as passionate concern for all of nature and, especially, to the path whereby humanity reestablishes a harmonious and balanced relationship with nature. This was expressed of old by the pre-manifestation image, *The Angel of Earth and the Angel of Humanity Walking Arm-In-Arm.*

This matter of the invisible soul of every form carries us back to the basis of the diviner's fundamental perceptions. Starting with what is closest to us, we cannot help but observe that each of us has a visible half and an invisible half. Further observation confirms that *everything* has a visible half and an invisible half. It goes without saying that the visible half is called the body and the invisible half, of course, the soul.

It is from this ages-old perception about the nature of appearance and reality that diviners originally grounded their art of seeing beneath the surface of the visible half in order to see the invisible half.

PART TWO

THE ROLE OF WILL

CHAPTER 1

SURRENDER

The greatest act of free will is to surrender to the One Will.

The modern industrial mind recoils from the suggestion that it abdicate its sovereign right to control its own destiny. If pressed, however, it has a difficult time justifying this position, given all the mistakes, missed opportunities and false hopes that have made up so many of the decision points in its lifetime. Conditioned since childhood to rationalize errors in judgement and to blame others for its missteps, the modern industrial mind either withdraws into shame and self-doubt or projects outward with distrust and certainty: "We are different than the animals in that we have free will and are not controlled by instinct," it clamors instinctively. Without any sense of irony, it watches the collective behavior of the species wreak havoc not only on itself, but on the very world it depends on for sustenance: unable to transcend its instinct for individual survival, it fails to exert the very free will required to secure the common good for humanity and nature.

For the older mind, the animistic mind, reality looks very different. It is a world in which things are *perfect in and of themselves*, even if not necessarily by the standards of human beings. Unable to see beyond the *synergistic horizon*, the modern industrial mind mistakes the apparent imperfections of the *parts* for the conjectured imperfection of the *Whole*.

The Whole is greater than the sum of its parts.

All Creation *flows* from its headwaters in the Original Void to its destination in the Oceanic Perfection. This *flowing* from origin to destination is the act of realizing the original vision of perfection. This *act* binding All Creation together in the moment-to-moment realization is the One Will, also called Divine Will. The original *vision* that set it all in motion is the One Purpose, also called Divine Intent.

The state of the *Whole* cannot be predicted by the state of the *parts*. This is what is called the *synergistic horizon*. So long as one identifies with the part, the illusion of separate selves inhabiting an imperfect universe persists. But once one identifies with the Whole, the *trance of separateness* is broken and one experiences the perfection of reality as a great chrysalis within which All Creation incubates: to identify with the Whole is to experience *The Imago*—the Living Being metamorphosing within the form of the physical universe. Born of all the mortal deaths in the universe, The Imago rises from the ashes of the eventual death of the physical universe itself: the transmuted lower soul of the manifestation realm, it carries the lives of all beings into its new incarnation of physical immortality.

With this recognition of the entirety of the physical universe from beginning to end as the *Lower Soul of Creation*, the One Spirit manifesting the universe reveals itself as the *Higher Soul of Creation*. The yoking of these *Two Souls* occurs in the fully individuated awareness of mortal-immortal being, whose presence unites the Heaven of eternity and the Earth of moments-in-time. As with individual souls, the *Lower Soul of Creation* is the *Memory of Time*, wherein nothing that ever exists is lost; similarly, the *Higher Soul of Creation* is the *Understanding of Eternity*, wherein Divine Intelligence incorporates the ever-reincarnating wisdom of the Ages.

As Above, So Below.

This view of reality depends utterly on attuning one's will to the Divine Will of eternal evolution—not just evolution of the parts, but of the Whole Itself. It is the alchemical view of Universal Transmutation, wherein the sum of all the mortal deaths of the individual parts is transcended in the immortal life of the Whole—a sacrifice made willingly as the Memory of every moment of time and every lifetime is preserved forever in the *Lower Soul of Creation*.

It is for this reason that it has long been said that the true view of reality depends on the death of the ego—called the Great Death, it is the transformative event in the diviner's evolution, as it breaks the identification with bodily survival and transcends it in an identification with the indestructible nature destined to survive all. This emergence of the Transcendental Ego coincides with the attunement of individual will to divine will—they are dependent on one another for their mutual arising.

Just as consciousness has a passive aspect and an active aspect, then, will has a human aspect and a divine aspect.

Consciousness is, Will does.

Consciousness is a limited form of awareness. It is the sum of the body's experiences. It exists; it perceives and it conceives. But it takes a *motive force*, a compelling desire, to move it into action. A rudimentary metaphor would have *consciousness* as the source of the sun's light and *will* as the *motive force* propelling the sun's light outward to illuminate the dark, warm the cold, and nourish life.

If *consciousness* is a cart laden with valuable objects, then *will* is the ox drawing it across the landscape of experience. Will, in other words, is *striving*: striving to get something, striving to avoid something, striving to make something, striving to destroy something, striving to change something, striving to be something.

Will is the motive force of *passive consciousness*. It strives to fulfill the desires of the habit mind. It strives to evade the aversions of the habit mind. So long as a person's identity is formed by the passive consciousness, the will pursues all the various strategies of physical self-interest.

Eradicating passive consciousness withdraws the will, however, creating an opening for *intent* to surface more distinctly as *active consciousness* comes to the foreground.

Will differs from Intent in this quintessential manner: Whereas Will is the motive force of passive consciousness, *Intent is the motive force of active consciousness*.

There is a clarity and purpose to intent that is reflective of the clarity and purposefulness of active consciousness. It *adds to the momentum* of ideas, values and visions as they move toward manifestation. It encourages, it collaborates, it forms alliances. It quite naturally and spontaneously moves in harmony with the intent of the One Spirit.

As active consciousness comes increasingly to the forefront of the lower soul's awareness, the habit will recedes, replaced by the individual's intent toward creativity, freedom and benevolence. Active consciousness evolves as its intent extends the limits of awareness and explores the glory of Creation.

This draws the lower soul into direct contact with the higher soul, resulting in their yoking during the individual's present lifetime. This coincides with the growing awareness of the presence of *Divine Intent,* also called *Universal Intent*. These two radical transformations are dependent on one another for their mutual arising.

This evolution is the manifestation of the saying, *The greatest act of free will is to surrender to the One Will*. The voluntary withdrawal of passive consciousness is, itself, an act of the intent of active consciousness—a recognition by the lower soul of its dissatisfaction with the identity formed around the habit mind of passive consciousness. As the *habit will* recedes, the intent emerges, reinforcing the growing identification with active consciousness, thereby paving the way for the yoking of the lower soul and higher soul. Out of this union, the Transcendental Ego comes to identify with the Universal Intent permeating All Creation.

The diviner-as-animist observes the natural world and sees that the sun nourishes all beings equally, that the rain nourishes all beings equally, that the soil nourishes all beings equally. From this, the transcendental ego emanates an intent wholly in harmony with the divine intent:

To Benefit All At The Same Time

Diviners participate as a kind of spiritual medicine, always attending to the needs of what is before them and sharing whatever of their resources might alleviate those needs. This is so both in the material world of the Life Realm and the spirit world of the Soul Realm—both in the manifestation realm of form and the pre-manifestation realm of images. The lower soul no longer wanders without guidance through the present lifetime—yoked with the higher soul, it *understands* the way of ascending and descending the Axis Mundi: by honing their intent to the white-hot light of Divine Fire, diviners *enter* the Soul Realm and *participate* in the ongoing creation of the manifestation realm.

This *act of entering* is a ritual of intent, which unites two streams of concentration into a single river of intent. The first is a single-minded concentration on a single thought one intuits is in harmony with Divine Intent, such as, *To Benefit All*. The second is a single-minded concentration on a whole-body sense of reverence for the perfecting momentum of Divine Intent. Fusing the two into a single unbroken intent breaks the *trance of separateness* fostered by the five senses, allowing the diviner to rend the veil and step into the Imaginal realm of the Spirit World.

Similarly, the *act of participating* is a ritual of intent, wherein the diviner encounters the image-symbols of *Psyche* and collaborates with other souls within that realm to focus their collective intent on *adding to the momentum* of beneficial symbols moving from the pre-manifestation realm into the manifestation realm. Diviners reach this degree of participation because they have cultivated a corresponding degree of *pure intent*, utterly lacking any ulterior motives of self-interest.

If *pure intent* is the sail of a great vessel, then *divine intent* is the wind that propels it across The Deep—across the living abyss of the Great Mystery whose depths cannot be plumbed nor expanse fathomed. Here, the diviner stands on the precipice of The Deep, witness to the arising of *new potential* emerging from the living engine of Creation. As intrinsically paradoxical as matter and anti-matter, this station is *The Uncreated*, the Great Void, the Absolute Nothingness from which All Creation arises. It is the Nonbeing that is the Well of Being, *The Uncreated* that is the source of *The Living Creation*. Out of its depths issues the *Coming Change* ever at work on the perpetual return of all things to *The One*. It can be said that this experience ritualizes a diviner's true initiation—*a vision of the Oracle suspended above The Abyss on its tripod seat*—for nowhere is the Oracle's presence felt so strongly as this, the Divine Dark that is the birthplace of Divine Fire.

Divine Intent carries the diviner to this place and Divine Intent carries the diviner away from this place, for it can be blinding to look too long into the sun. But for the diviner, the intensity of the experience is in inverse proportion to its briefness—the actuality of being present at the Furnace of Creation burns an afterimage into the *imaginal soul* that forever remains the touchstone by which the diviner recognizes worth.

At this juncture, *pure intention* identifies with the *imaginal soul*, uniting in a single awareness called the *intentional body*: part *psychic substance* and part *motive force*, the intentional body roams free and unencumbered within the pre-manifestation realm of the World Soul. It is the "face" of the diviner therein, in the sense that it assumes the form of the image-symbol reflective of the diviner's nature and in that form participates with other souls through their own image-symbols.

In the course of that participation, diviners engage in the practice of *Dreaming* in order to fulfill one of the traditional functions of the role of shaman in pre-industrial communities—that of lengthening periods of good fortune and shortening periods of misfortune. This they do through the agency of the *intentional body* in collaboration with other souls, focusing their collective intent on *adding to the momentum* of beneficial image-symbols in the pre-manifestation realm of the World Soul. Like the diviners themselves, these image-symbols are themselves souls—an actuality unchanged upon their emergence from the Dreamtime into the manifestation realm of full materialization. An actuality, too, that is universally recognized in pre-industrial cultures, whose treatment of all forms as sacred vessels of their respective souls does not fail to inspire the modern industrial mind to aspire to greater sensitivity to the Spirit of Nature.

CHAPTER 2

RECEPTIVITY

The whole of the art is based on Listening.

Will does not listen. It acts. It does. It pursues, especially the objects of the habit mind: anxiety, lust, dominance. It strives to have, to hold on to, to become. It reacts to perceived need.

So long as one identifies with the *habit mind*, the will occupies the greater part of one's attention through its strivings, accomplishments and frustrations. This is not a state of mind conducive to divination.

The diviner cannot *want* something from the divination. Not even for the querent to benefit from or understand the Oracle's message. And especially not for some form of appreciation or recognition from the querent—their attention, like the diviner's own, should be solely fixed on the Oracle's message and their response to it.

The ability to act without self-interest, without striving, comes with the emergence of active consciousness and the submergence of passive consciousness. This shift in awareness presents the diviner with the opportunity to transcend the will through the practice of *mindlessness*.

Viewing the *mind moment* as the present state of consciousness, it can be envisioned as a field of awareness, a Field of Thought, in which individual thoughts arise and pass away. These individual thoughts are called "inner actions," regardless of whether they are willed thoughts or unwilled thoughts. Just as a field of grass is tranquil on a calm day, still the scene is altered by a butterfly flitting through, or a bird flying by, or a rabbit hopping past, or a fox trotting along. The field of thought is like the open field of grass on a calm day and the animals coming and going through the scene are like the individual thoughts arising and passing away. The practice of mindlessness involves sustaining longer and longer periods of experiencing the tranquil clearing without the intrusion of inner actions.

Mindlessness is the Field of Thought not thinking thoughts.

Such is the source of *Listening*.

Generally speaking, people either endure the distress of the habit mind's passive consciousness or they avoid it by distracting themselves with a constant stream of music, mass media and social contact. But there is essentially no difference between these two responses—it is like the difference between listening either to the inside of the machine or the outside of the machine, and so being unable to hear the living voice of that which calls from beyond the stars and beneath the sea. The voice of spirit does not drown out human will—it waits to be welcomed by a wiser and nobler awareness.

The diviner's identification with active consciousness lays the foundation for just such an awareness, yet even active consciousness has to stop and revert to stillness if the voice of spirit is to be heard clearly. Just because it produces creative, constructive and collaborative thoughts, does not mean that active consciousness is itself the voice of spirit. It is, however, inspired by spirit.

Stopping active consciousness and allowing it to revert to stillness opens awareness to the state of mindlessness called *receptivity*, or *original listening*. During these moments, when consciousness is interrupted, the voice of spirit rushes in with the messages that active consciousness needs at that time in order to create, construct and collaborate. In this sense, diviners divine themselves, listening to the voice of spirit and then reverting back to active consciousness in order to interpret spirit's guidance into thought, word or act. Prolonged acts of creativity, construction and collaboration incorporate many such shifts back and forth between *receptive listening* and *active interpreting*.

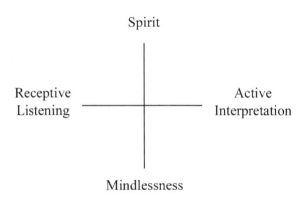

It is at the intersection of these four elements that the diviner crosses the threshold of authentic communion with the Oracle. The meaning of its symbols are suddenly clear and it is as though the Oracle speaks directly through the diviner. This manifests most expressly in the natural and spontaneous manner with which the diviner construes from the Oracle's symbols a narrative that perfectly bridges the querent's question and the Oracle's reply—all the ritual aspects of the act of divination that occurs in the sacred space described by the intersection wherein *Mindlessness* calls in the *Voice of Spirit*, which is revealed to *Receptive Listening* and ultimately rendered comprehensible by *Active Interpretation*.

Spirit fills every vacuum.

Just as Nature rushes in to fill every empty niche in an environment, Spirit rushes in to fill every empty Field of Thought. Welcomed in by the practice of *stopping and listening*, Spirit guides diviners' footsteps in the Life Realm as well as the Soul Realm. As diviners walk the path of Spirit more and more, they walk in the footsteps of the elder souls and cannot help but absorb the wisdom of the ancients' experiences and incorporate it into their own thoughts, feelings, intentions and actions.

CHAPTER 3

KAIROS

The greatest part of wisdom lies in timing.

To arrive ahead of time is no better than arriving late.

To do the right thing at the wrong time is no better than doing the wrong thing.

To say the right thing at the wrong time is no better than saying the wrong thing.

To act without any real feeling of the underlying harmony of Creation is to decide at random and to act at random.

To act without any real feeling of the underlying perfection of Creation is to risk losing everything.

To act without any real feeling of the holiness of All Creation is to risk desecrating one's own soul.

Wisdom is simple and easy—it just depends on following the natural metamorphosis of things. The natural metamorphosis of things is the manifestation of the underlying harmony of creation, the underlying perfection of Creation and the holiness of All Creation.

To be aligned with the underlying harmony of Creation is to consciously sense the beauty and elegance of the way that matter, life and spirit flow together in a great river of change, ever evolving into new forms and relationships. This intrinsic harmony is considered the reality underlying the world of appearances as perceived by the five senses— it establishes the order, inexplicable at its smallest and largest dimensions, by which the predictable and the unpredictable give rise to mist-shrouded mountains, the ecstatic flight of larks, the slow-motion grace of whales, the cave art of prehistoric artists, the relationship between insects and blossoms and between the tides and the moon and, concretely, between every single thing and every other in the whole of nature. Consciously sensing the underlying harmony of Creation, the diviner feels themselves *on the path*, true to their compass heading, a leaf on the river of Being carried homeward to the sea.

To be aligned with the underlying perfection of Creation is to consciously sense the *as-is-ness* of all things. Also called the *suchness* of all things, it reveals itself as *perfect-as-is*, or *perfect-in-itself*, absolutely independent of human values and mores. To perceive every moment in time as perfect as a flower in full bloom is to experience the full mystery of eternity, for the flower in full bloom is both the apex of the individual evolution as well as the point at which it moves toward death. This is to say that every moment-in-time is like a wave, suspended forever at its crest—perfect in its form as the culmination of the entire ocean's momentum and perfect in its inevitable break and rushing back into the sea. Diviners move from wave to wave, consciously sensing the immensity of the ocean and its radical unconcern for the safety of those who enter it without learning its ways. Surrendering their individual will, preferences, desires, comfort and judgements, diviners completely cease asking themselves, *What is wrong with this picture?* Rather, they train themselves to look at their world and ask, *What is right with this picture?* Similarly, they cease completely asking themselves, *What is missing here?* in favor of the mystic's, *What is present here?*

To be aligned with the holiness of All Creation is to consciously sense the entirety of the Form, the Formless and

97

the Unchanging as the living embodiment of the One Spirit. Diviners are not limited to a range of emotions that reinforce the solidity of an individual identity somehow separate from the whole of existence. Rather, they learn, from their explorations along the World Axis and in particular the World Soul, to *step outside themselves* into the fuller experience of existence, identifying with *the ecstatic life*. The consequence of the *Mystical Union* of the individual soul and the One Soul is a shattering of every illusion of separateness from The Divine. Holy beings, walking on holy ground, breathing holy air, drawing from the holy well, warmed by the holy fire—the bubble bursts and lo and behold, it is the same air inside and out. This *reunion* of inside and outside that occurs when the membrane of separateness bursts marks the return to the Act of Creation, when the Divine Seed of living potential takes root in the living ground of the Divine Void—the *act of continuing creation* that never stalls nor ceases. At this point, the diviner fully realizes their own divine nature and accepts responsibility for treating all other beings as divine.

Divination, then, from this perspective, is a ritual act wherein the Oracle sets things back on *their divine path*.

Every thing, every being, every soul, is understood as a unique Idea of the One Mind: as such, each is an emanation of the One as it emerges into the *Mind Realm*.

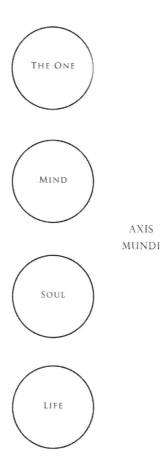

Each Eternal Idea then progressively *densifies* as it further emanates into the Soul Realm and the Life Realm. Upon full manifestation in the Life Realm, each thing, each being, each soul, steps onto *their divine path*, which is their individual *return to the One.*

This perspective of the Oracle is one that the diviner must ever hold in the forefront of their awareness, for it speaks of a path that spans lifetimes. It speaks to the soul, reminding it of its true essence as an Eternal Idea of the One Mind, pointing to *their divine path* in the secret language of living symbols. This means that the Oracle's message is never restricted to the querent's present lifetime. It also means that the trans-lifetime message is delivered in a form that the querent's consciousness may not register. And, it further means that the diviner must take the greatest pains to relay the Oracle's message in the clearest manner possible and interpret it without any hint of personal opinion: the diviner must have absolute trust that the divination is like the song of the sea echoing in the conch shell, calling each home.

Diviners must master *the way of noninterference* if they are to benefit others. This means that they must eradicate the hubris of their individual will—they must confront the unfathomable nature of existence, experiencing the Great Mystery authentically and coming to grips with the fact that nothing in the human realm is ultimately knowable. To admit to oneself and others that the *order of predictability and unpredictability* moves in mysterious ways, assuring that fate is dependent upon unforeseeable accidents and coincidences, is to humble oneself before the altar of Truth. The diviner who tells the querent what decision to make has failed. The diviner who predicts the future for a querent has failed. The diviner who knows what is best for the querent has failed.

The *way of noninterference* centers around the diviner's trust in the querent's natural path of metamorphosis being guided by the underlying harmony of Creation. It also centers around the diviner's recognition of the underlying perfection of the querent-as-they-are per the perspective of the Oracle. And, further, it also centers around the diviner's reverence for the holiness of All Creation and an unwillingness to dishonor the *querent's divine path*. All in all, the *way of noninterference* demands of the diviner the highest degree of neutrality, suspended judgement and good will in every thought, word and act.

Diviners embody the ancient wisdom teachings within the historical era in which they live.

History is what happens between Golden Ages. This is because during a Golden Age, nothing appears noteworthy. Nothing appears exceptional. The natural spontaneity of individual and collective metamorphosis expresses itself in the underlying harmony, perfection and holiness of everyday life. Civilization attains balance and harmony within itself and with Nature. Although the continuing creation of all things results in the ongoing betterment of all things, there is no sense of progress nor striving for progress. There is no sense of wisdom, because it has been internalized and incorporated in the thoughts, feelings, words and acts of everyday life.

But when the harmony and balance are disrupted and a Golden Age comes to an end, its lifeway and worldview are recorded by forward-looking individuals despairing of the suffering to come. And so, the wisdom teachings come into being.

Diviners think and feel and speak and act as if they live in a Golden Age. This is because they see beneath the surface of appearances into the underlying harmony, perfection and holiness of every moment in time. They are not *less* adapted to the time in which they live, but *more so*, because they treat it as sacred and take the greatest interest in its inner workings. By living in this manner, moreover, they add to the momentum of the coming Golden Age.

Seeing beneath the surface of appearances can be likened to coming upon a lake and seeing the clouds in the sky reflected in its surface. At first, the sky's reflection is all that can be seen. But by staring at the nearest edge of the lake and *re-focusing vision past the reflection,* the lakebed beneath the surface suddenly opens to view.

A mirage is a real thing—it is just not what it looks like.

Although the word "mirage" is often used to connote an illusion, a mirage is actually heat waves rising off the ground—it is a *real* phenomenon. It is just not the oasis it *looks* like.

Just because something is an illusion, in other words, does not mean it isn't real. The world of appearances of the five senses is real, but temporary, whereas the underlying harmony is real, but permanent. What makes the world of appearances an illusion is the fact that it is not the permanent world of spirit—that it will one day come to an end.

Seeing through illusion, then, is a matter of correct perception and *not a matter of something being unreal.* The illusion lies in one's own perception mistaking something transitory for something eternal.

The art of *seeing through* illusion into the reality of Creation is similar to the water diviner finding water hidden beneath the surface of the ground. It is not an intellectual exercise nor a willed perception. It is, rather, an attunement to the invisible, inaudible, intangible *essence* shining through appearances. The water diviner has cultivated a new sense organ, one that is sensitized to the essence of water far below the threshold of the sensitivity of the five senses — rather than going out in search of water, dowsers allow *their own essence* to be pulled by the essence of water. This follows the ancient alchemical dictum of *Like attracts Like,* or, gold attracts gold, which is to say, essence attracts essence.

The essence of the water dowser is already attuned to the essence of water ahead of time. The essence of the diviner is already attuned to the essence of the underlying harmony ahead of time. It is the diviner's cultivation of a new sense organ that sensitizes them to the *pull* of the underlying harmony and its *intersections of coincidences*, that most mysterious manifestation of the order of predictability and unpredictability.

There is a place where the essence of the underlying harmony meets the essence of the world of appearances — where the essence of the underlying reality meets the essence of the material world. It is a borderland where nondifferentiation meets differentiation, giving rise to a third realm, so to speak, of overlapping lines of possibilities. Where these lines of the predictable and the unpredictable *merge in a moment in time*, a coincidence is born.

Coincidences appear as a rupture in the order of predictability. Yet they are the inevitable consequence of the order of unpredictability intruding on the order of predictability — for that is precisely what a coincidence is: the predictable and the unpredictable happening at the same time. Unpredictability alone is not a coincidence — it is only when it is paired with the predictable that coincidence arises.

Coincidences are openings in the otherwise closed course of predictable opportunities. Without them, life would be an endless chain of fated events, each utterly predictable based on what preceded it. A world governed only by the unpredictable would be no better, of course, as it would be nothing but a random chaos of unrelated events with no sense of cause-and-effect. But when these two orders converge in their *intersections of coincidences*, they create unexpected and often unimaginable opportunities for bettering situations.

It is their nature not only to appear unexpectedly, but to disappear just as unexpectedly—they arrive on the scene spontaneously and they withdraw just as spontaneously. Not only are they short-lived, but veiled, as well, from the sight of those not prepared for their appearance. Diviners, however, recognize such opportunities for what they are, as they are sensitized *ahead of time* to the inner workings of the underlying harmony's order of predictability and unpredictability.

Because they appear to rupture the order of predictability, coincidences shatter the illusion of a routine of normalcy governing life. This grants them the status of numinous events, separated from the rest of normal life by their unearthly character—and this is especially so because each coincidence of the predictable and unpredictable can occur at one and only one moment in time. It is its unique placement in time that accounts for the sense of extraordinariness attributed to the coincidence—and makes arriving at the *intersection of coincidences* at the right moment such an art.

Kairos is an ancient Greek word best rendered as *the magically right moment* to do something, to say something, to be somewhere. In mystic circles, it is seen as the moment in which the Divine takes action in the world. Such an *appointed time* is seen as an intersection of eternity and a moment in time. It is the precise right moment—of aim and timing—to release the arrow and hit a moving target.

The greatest part of wisdom is discerning the emerging *kairos* ahead of time, to sense the coming *intersection of coincidences* in order to enter the moment already at one with the warp and woof of the hidden loom of destiny beneath the surface of appearances. Sometimes the *kairos* can be felt about to irrupt in the next moment. Sometimes the *kairos* can be felt gaining momentum to irrupt years away. But there is always a sense of the *inevitable* about the *kairos*, a *rightness* about a change that acts as a turning point in events and lives.

Divinations are coincidences.

They are rituals in which the order of predictability and unpredictability converge with the order of eternity and time.

Divinations, then, create a ritual space for the manifestation of the *Grand Convergence of Kairos* —

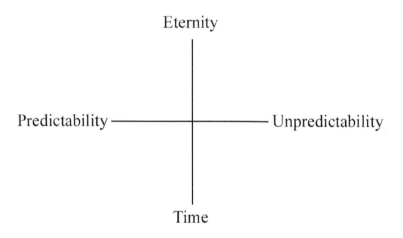

GRAND CONVERGENCE OF KAIROS

Diviners occupy the center of the ritual space, so to speak, joining its various elements in an attitude of *reverential welcoming*: divinations have a ritualistic and therefore predictable form; divinations incorporate randomness (the unpredictable casting of coins, drawing of cards, moment of birth, etc.) into their readings; diviners have an established attunement with the Oracle in its spatiality of eternity; and, the diviner waits for the magically-charged moment-in-time to conduct the divination proper.

As the aware receptacle of these four elements, diviners hold open a sacred space of living potential wherein Divine Intent ensures the querent's feet are set solidly upon *their divine path*.

The diviner's focus on timing is of the utmost importance in keeping the *querent's divine path* the first and foremost concern of the divination.

Such a focus embodies the ancients' most personal advice to their descendants:

The greatest tragedy in life
is to arrive at someone else's destination.

PART THREE

STEPPING OUTSIDE TIME

.

CHAPTER 1

REFUGE

"What will you be after you die?"

The Aboriginal shaman gazed at me intently, waiting for my reply. I had to confess that I had never thought of the matter that way and then remarked that I was interested to know how he answered that question.

"Out there in the bush," he replied, pointing to the vast Outback desert, "there's a ravine with a stream that comes out of a hill and runs down between red boulders and white ghost gum trees. In the morning, there's a breeze that flows up the ravine and in the evening, there's a breeze that flows down the ravine. After I die, I am going to be that breeze that flows down the ravine in the evening."

"That way," I replied, "you'll be with all your family and loved ones who are the stream that comes out of the hill and the red boulders and the white ghost gum trees and the breeze that flows up the ravine in the morning."

"So shall it be," he responded solemnly.[1]

---

[1] See my book, *In the Oneness of Time: The Education of a Diviner*, Larson Publications, regarding this and related episodes.

The ancients understood the creative power of the soul. It is, after all, from the pre-manifestation Soul Realm that the material forms of the manifestations of the Life Realm are created. Indeed, one's own physical body is just such a manifestation of one's soul.

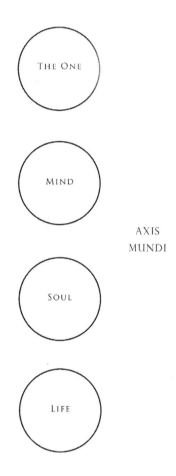

But they also understood that the spatiality of the Soul Realm is not restricted to pre-manifestation image-symbols. The *substance of psyche* contains entire *domains* produced by generations of souls creating a refuge for their after-death existence.

In other words: while the secret of manifestation in the Life Realm lies in adding to the momentum of the pre-manifestation image-symbols within the Soul Realm, the reverse is not only true as well, but is actually more often practiced.

Souls living in the realm of manifestation form and sustain domains within the Soul Realm.

These *domains* are the result of reverential concentration on image-symbols of Paradise by millions of mortal souls over thousands of years.

It is the *sustained collective intent* of mortal souls in the Life Realm that render their cultural visions of Paradise into spiritual realities within the Soul Realm.

Elder wisdom traditions, rooted in an animistic worldview, create *domains* (such as that at the beginning of this chapter) of an after death Paradise steeped in nature and lineage veneration.

Newer religions likewise create *domains* of Paradise reflecting their history and culture, such as a Western vision like *Heaven*, or an Eastern vision, like *Pure Land*. Most of the newer religions also create related *domains* of after death punishment, such as *Hell*, which are occupied by souls suffering from guilt and shame.

Composed of the same *substance of psyche* as the individual soul, these *domains* have a spatial nature no less tangible or infinite as the physical universe itself. As realms within the Soul Realm, these *domains* are the product of many generations of people placing their soul's intent into an everlasting refuge in the afterlife. As many people from many cultures attest upon dying for a short time and then being revived, these are real places, occupied by other souls and filled with greater wonders than they had imagined. This last point exhibits the substantial nature of *objective psyche*, demonstrating that the *domain* is not a product of the individual's consciousness, but results from the collective intent of many souls from many time periods with many different visions of the same Paradise.

What will you be after you die? is the eternal question posed by the immortal soul. Generations of people answer that question by concentrating on a common vision of Paradise with the faith that *that domain* is the destination of their soul after death: *So shall it be*.

An important caveat needs to be inserted here, in reminder of the *yoking* of the lower soul with the higher soul in its metamorphosis and return to *The One*. In other words, not all souls enter the Soul Realm after death of the physical body or come to dwell in the vision of Paradise of their spiritual belief. Some follow the path of *mystical union* all the way to the soul's immediate and ultimate dissolution into the oceanic communion of *The One*.

Souls enter the *domains* of the Soul Realm after death because they desire a refuge within which their individual identity lives on. Some never leave. Some, as image-symbols themselves, eventually reincarnate as new bodily manifestations in the Life Realm. Some eventually leave to explore the rest of the Soul Realm. And, some eventually return to the path of mystical union and its reintegration of the individual and universal in *The One*.

Some elder wisdom traditions, however, illuminate a pathway to the soul's refuge *before death*. This is particularly so in the case of peoples who have suffered the loss of homeland and lifeway due to the encroachment of other cultures. The poverty of their material lives is in indirect proportion to the richness of their spiritual lives: they maintain a tradition whereby their soul consciously shifts into the Soul Realm and takes refuge in their *domain* while their living body still inhabits the manifestation realm. Such a practice makes a difficult life more bearable, reassures the practitioner of a joyous afterlife, and adds the practitioner's intent to the ancestors' in the creating and sustaining of the *domain*.

It is a practice that has much in common with that of *spirit journeying, spiritual cleansings, and soul retrievals.* Healers and shamans from elder cultures have long sent the *intentional body* into the Soul Realm for the purpose of benefiting others or the community as a whole. This is not something accomplished with conscious awareness bound to linear time—without the capacity to step outside their body into the eternal Spirit World, practitioners cannot work with the image-symbols necessary for spiritual transformation and reconciliation.

The Spirit World is the same as the Soul Realm—and the Imaginal, the Bardo, the Nagual, the Dreamtime, and so on—but is generally experienced as a vast landscape of landmarks, to be sure, but also more open to spontaneous shifts of scene, atmosphere and inhabitants. Its *domains* are so strongly identified with a particular Paradise that they seem to stand alone, apart from the rest of the *Realm of Psyche*.

In this vein, it is instructive to note that traditional teachings state that there are *individual domains*, equally autonomous in nature, created by souls of exceptional knowledge, wisdom and intent. To encounter such souls is to gain much impetus on one's *own divine path*.

CHAPTER 2

ENLIGHTENMENT

On a dark, moonless, starless night, a single lightning bolt splits the dark, illuminating the entire landscape for an instant of eternity. It is an instant imprinted on the soul, indelible and unforgettable, forever overlaid upon the shadow world of appearances. But it is not an illumination of all the things in the world—it is an illumination of all the relationships between the things in the world. To see the relationships between things is to see the essential nature of the inner workings of Creation. To see the inner workings of Creation is to be at one with the One Mind.

This is why lineage teachers are fond of saying: No one can know everything, but anyone can understand everything.

There are only so many relationships between things. Because of this, they are archetypal in nature. To see these in their entirety is to realize one's own participation in the archetypal level of reality. To participate in the archetypal level of reality is to ascend the World Axis to the *Mind Realm*. Here, in the realm of the Eternal Ideas, the diviner directly encounters the One Mind. In this experience, the diviner's mind is opened to its fullest potential by the influx of the living archetypes of the One Mind. This is called *Mind-to-mind transmission*. It is also called the *Second Death*, because whereas the First Death was that of the ego-identity and the birth of the Transcendental Ego, the Second Death is that of the Transcendental Ego and the birth of *aware light*.

Sloughing off both body and soul, awareness permeates space without form or substance: unbound and uncloaked, aware light *no longer abides anywhere*. This is what is called *the site of enlightenment*.

Many are the moments when the lightning bolt of enlightenment flashes, but too rare are the moments when a receptive mind perceives it. In this sense, the receptive mind that fully *realizes* the lightning of awakening is called *thunder*. For this reason, the moment of authentic enlightenment is called *Lightning and Thunder arriving at once*.

Of course, an enlightened state of mind is not necessary for a diviner to perform beneficial divinations. But every divination provides the opportunity for *lightning and thunder to arrive simultaneously*. And this is true not just for the querent but the diviner, as well: divinatory space is a sacred wellspring of infinite possibilities.

So many moments of missed recognition of the *lightning flash* occur because the modern industrial mind has mythologized the awakened state as something rare and nearly impossible to achieve. Yet, the elder wisdom traditions treated enlightenment as the normal and natural metamorphosis of awareness—it simply required the right circumstances and timing to produce the *receptive awareness* able to perceive the transmission of Mind. This receptive awareness is much more common than is generally believed; there are many more enlightened people alive at any time than popularly recognized—such individuals do not seek recognition nor do they take up actively teaching. Nonetheless, they inspire and encourage those around them with unadorned wisdom and generosity of spirit.

The natural course of the soul's evolution is one of alchemical transmutation. The first step, following the ancient formula, *Separate To Unite*, is burning off the dross of the habit mind. The second step, following the ancient formula, *The Wind Nourishes It In Its Womb*, is refining the gold of *active consciousness*. The third step, following the ancient formula, *As Above, So Below*, is yoking the lower soul and the higher soul. The fourth step, following the ancient formula, *Like Attracts Like*, is allowing awareness to be drawn into the One Mind. In this manner is ordinary consciousness transmuted into the *Philosopher's Stone* of aware light.

The modern industrial mind finds little use for such talk of intangible hypotheticals. But the elder wisdom traditions found the path of natural and spontaneous metamorphosis in the time-tested *practice of nature mysticism*. The alchemical steps of transformation, in other words, occur naturally and spontaneously to the individual engaging Nature as the living body of Spirit. Such an engagement quiets the mind, cultivates thought, recovers the higher self, and accepts dissolution into the Whole as part and parcel of the cycle of Life.

In this regard, it must be recalled that *the first enlightened person had no teacher, no teachings, no predecessor.*

From the lineage teachers' perspective, the enlightened mind is merged completely with the Mind of Heaven, with Eternity, with the Timeless.

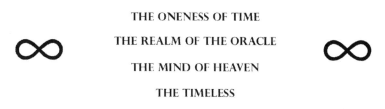

THE ONENESS OF TIME

THE REALM OF THE ORACLE

THE MIND OF HEAVEN

THE TIMELESS

PAST							PRESENT							FUTURE		
MOMENT OF TIME	MOMENT OF TIME	MOMENT OF TIME	MOMENT OF TIME	MOMENT OF TIME	MOMENT OF TIME	MOMENT OF TIME	MOMENT OF TIME	MOMENT OF TIME	MOMENT OF TIME	MOMENT OF TIME	MOMENT OF TIME	MOMENT OF TIME	MOMENT OF TIME	MOMENT OF TIME	MOMENT OF TIME	MOMENT OF TIME

This means that in the spatial realm of the Timeless, there is no "before" or "after" or even "generations." It is always, then, *the first generation.* And each individual awakened on the path of self-liberation *is* the first enlightened person. This also means that each individual has no teacher, no teachings, no predecessors, on the path of enlightenment.

The path of nature mysticism holds awareness in the embrace of innocence and uncontrived receptivity: one becomes aware of the One Mind and is naturally and spontaneously catapulted to the Mind Realm, a distinct drop of Idea returned to the oceanic Mind of Heaven.

This is called the short path to stepping outside time.

From this perspective, it is said that *Enlightenment is easy—returning to the world is hard.*

This is why it is traditionally said that a person should take a long time to integrate the enlightenment experience before ever trying to express it. One difficulty is that one's awareness has experienced eternity, a view so radically different from being immersed in time that it borders on inhuman. Another is that the understanding gleaned from eternity requires wisdom and empathy to be adapted to the historical era in which the person lives. A third is that the person's awareness is now twofold—timebound and eternal: the timebound half cultivates a personality in keeping with the person's circumstances and temperament, while the eternal half squats like a statue in an antediluvian ruins, its mind, words and acts all equally impenetrable.

This eternal half resembles nothing so much as a boulder of gold in the midst of a river: Ages pass and wash over it but it remains unchanged. It is an ancient being with its own memory and understanding, both at one with the personality and apart from it. When it moves, though, in speech or action, its effects ripple and echo across lifetimes, bringing light to darkness, relief to sorrow, meaning to confusion, and passion to world-weariness.

Those who are celebrated as authentically enlightened beings are those who allow the eternal half to break through the veil of the personality and express itself as directly as circumstances permit or warrant. Those who choose to "hide their light under a bushel" do so in order to remain true to *their divine path*: people who awaken early and easily generally have other enlightened lives behind them and find that anonymity in this lifetime serves their trans-lifetime project best.

All other facets of the practice aside, diviners stand at the center of the sacred space of the *Grand Convergence of Kairos*, suspended weightless between the dual *orders of Creation*.

What better place for the receptive vessel to wait to be filled? By *receptive vessel* is meant the open, welcoming mind devoid of preconceptions or expectations of the nature of what is awaited. Inevitably, it arrives: at first, one plays host to the welcomed guest but once it has taken up lodging, it plays host to one's place as guest.

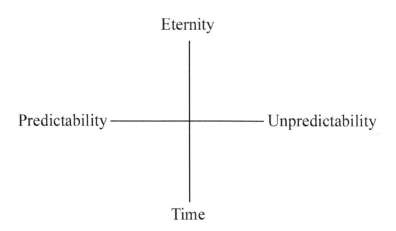

The moment of enlightenment arrives on its own, at its own magically right moment of *Kairos*, perfectly balanced at the omnipresent intersection of the dual *axes of Creation*. From this *inner void*, the ancestors' blessing to their descendants echoes still :

Awaken Early

Find Lifelong Allies

CHAPTER 3

THE STEP

An ancient axiom sets the stage for the diviner's step outside time:

The more time one spends with the Oracle,
the more one's mind becomes like the mind of the Oracle.

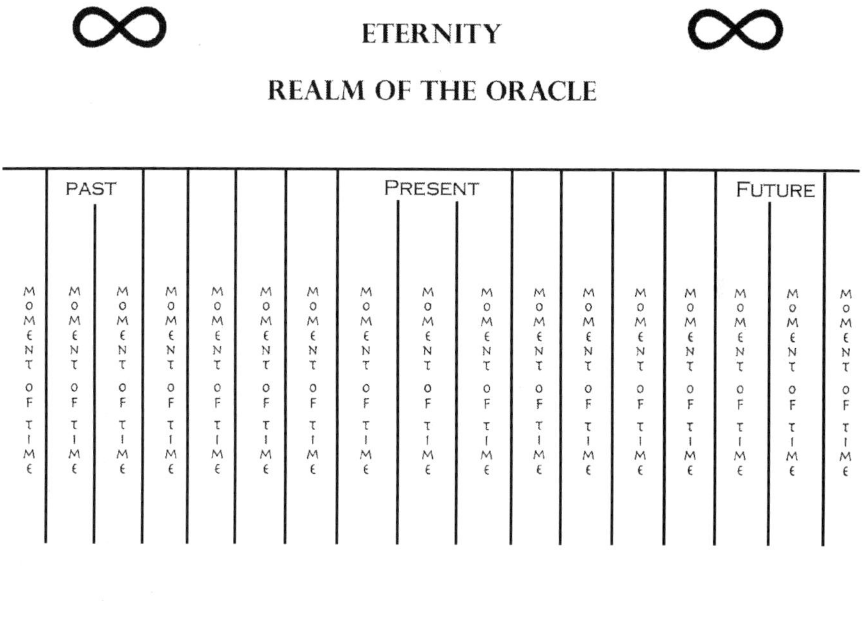
ETERNITY
REALM OF THE ORACLE
PAST
PRESENT
FUTURE
MOMENT OF TIME

To step outside time is to step into eternity and into the realm of the Oracle. Diviners are ideally poised to take this step consciously, as they have rigorously attuned themselves to the Oracle and its symbolic language. This means they are accustomed to the Soul Realm and its universe of image-symbols moving in a constant roil of transformation.

But awareness influenced by the human experience of this lifetime maintains its view of the linear passage of states and events, even when immersed in the Dreamtime of the World Soul. Even the chaotification of the Imaginal state's nondifferentiated ocean of mutual transmutation of image-symbols maintains its orderly progression of one thing becoming another. Even within the *domains* of the Soul Realm, the refuges provide the familiarity of cause-and-effect events, regardless of their dreamlike nature.

In other words, awareness has not yet stepped *outside the illusion of linear change and into the reality of the unchanging simultaneity of eternity.*

The Oracle is the *speaking* of the One Spirit, the One Mind, *The One.* It is the voice of the *single thought* by which all things are steered together. Creation, in this sense, is like a great ship holding all things and all times, with a single hand upon the tiller on the ocean of eternity.

Its realm is the *Oneness of Time*, wherein all things in Creation *happen at the same time*. However, because awareness has stepped into the Great Simultaneity and is now part and parcel of it, the illusion of ideas, images and events dissolves into the reality of a *single thought*. This is the result of the nondual nature of awareness once the subject-object dichotomy is dissolved: awareness cannot view eternity from the perspective of an observer because it is now eternity itself, just as a drop of water returned to the sea is now the sea itself.

But the drop of water dispersed back into the sea is intimately connected to the tides and currents all the way across the ocean. Similarly, awareness newly entered into eternity is likewise at one with everything in the *single body of thought*. Within the "ship of eternity" is the whole of the timebound universe contained, everything bound by the law of inertia—but the "ship of eternity" itself knows no inertia: it never comes to rest. It has no mass, it is pure thought, aware light, self-originated outside any field of resistance that might slow or bring it to a stop.

It is a single instant forever.

Nothing can prepare awareness for the immensity of perfection in the span of the instantaneous blossoming of Creation. An awareness influenced by the human experience of this lifetime cannot help but imagine eternity as a vast unending expanse of time that somehow does not pass. But the reality is far different: as the water drop of awareness disperses throughout the ocean, it finds that it is *entangled* with every other drop of awareness in a way more immediately physical than ideational or visual — everything is *already one*, much as one's hand moves as soon as one thinks about moving it. There is no time because there is no distance between things. It is all *already known* and the grandeur of perfection of the *single thought* fills the whole with a sense of meaningful purpose that imbues its every idea, image and event with its sacred intent. In the infinity of the dark void, Eternity is the Divine Fire.

Once awareness steps into eternity and *consciously* becomes one with the *single thought*, it recognizes, of course, that it has *always* been so—but in a manner completely obscured by the veil of time. So compelling is the experience of *change* within the timebound realm, that the most jarring sense of stepping into eternity is immersion in *the unchanging*. People understand that a human dream that lasts only a second may seem to last many hours, but still, it is difficult for the timebound mind to conceive of a single thought that lasts an eternity. A single divine thought of the magnitude of Creation lasts an eternal dream of moments-in-time.

Thought requires a *Thinking*, which then requires a *Thinker*, which further requires a *Being*. This *Being of Thought* has created its own body—the physical universe of time.

The *Being of Thought* moreover requires *awareness*, which in turn, requires self-awareness.

The self-aware aspect of the *Being of Thought* knows its own unchanging thought, but likewise knows the universe of time and change that it has created.

This awareness faces two directions at once: one face is moving, the other face is unmoving. It is said to be moving when it faces the universe of time and change. It is said to be unmoving when it faces eternity and the unchanging.

It is this self-aware aspect of the *Being of Thought* that speaks through *the Oracle*.

The ancient axiom bears repeating:

The more time one spends with the Oracle,
the more one's mind becomes like the mind of the Oracle.

At first, the diviner learns the skills necessary to conduct the divination. This stage is preliminary to the person thinking of themselves as a *diviner*. It involves learning the form of the divination and a growing familiarity with its symbols. For many, this is a matter of mere curiosity and treated as little more than a party game.

For those who actively pursue the act of divination with a sense of dedication and reverence, the second stage involves a deep study of the symbols, eventually resulting in a personal sense of being a diviner able to interpret the Oracle's symbols for themselves and others. Even at this relatively early stage of the practice, diviners experience the distinct sensation of having the Oracle speak through them. It is at this point in the practice that diviners perceive why the ancient diviners were called priests and priestesses, for the sacredness of all things is a compelling presence in their lives—as is the recognition of the necessity to concretize the practice as one of self-purification and self-cultivation.

The third stage finds the diviner conducting divinations that, in essence, cannot be said to be qualitatively different than shamanic cleansings, spirit journeying, soul retrievals, and other forms of spiritual healing. At this stage, every act in life seems to be a divination, a *seeing through the illusion* of the world of appearances—and an immediate at-one-ment with the *world-as-text* and the essential meaning of its symbols. The *diviner-as-animist* perceives the soul of every form within the manifestation realm, including the written and spoken word.

The last and fourth stage: the diviner has conducted enough divinations, both for themselves and others, that they begin to see the world the way the Oracle sees it. This is a kind of borderland sensation, as though one stands straddling the threshold between the moment-in-time and eternity—as though one stands straddling the threshold between one's own mind and the mind of the Oracle. Far from being a conceptual experience of one's own thoughts, this stage of the practice opens the gate to sharing the thoughts of the Oracle. There is not even a hair's-breadth of distance between sharing the thoughts of the Oracle and *dissolving back into the oceanic single thought.* In other words, breaking down the subject-object duality between oneself and the Oracle draws one into the nonduality of eternity.

This is called the long path of stepping outside time.

CHAPTER 4

SYMBOLIC VISION

Mystical traditions proclaim clearly: *Everything is God.*

Not "God is everything," but *Everything is God.* The difference is essential to the experience of mystical union with the One Spirit. "God is everything," while true, points to the Whole as the manifestation of the Creative Spirit. *Everything is God*, on the other hand, points to the divinity within every individual manifestation.

To consciously accept that one is a divine being in the midst of a universe of divine beings is to adopt the worldview of the mystical tradition. To consciously act as a divine being treating every other individual manifestation as a divine being is to embody the ethics of the mystical tradition.

From this perspective, every individual manifestation is a symbol of its origin in the creative act of the One Spirit. Each carries within it the *divine intent* of The One in its emanations of *eternal idea* in the Mind Realm, *immortal soul* in the Soul Realm, and *living symbol* in the Life Realm.

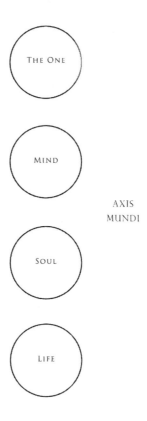

In this way, every individual manifestation is a link in a chain of *meaning* that leads directly back to The One and its Act of Creation.

It is *symbolic vision* that actively follows that chain of meaning back up the World Axis, from the *living symbol* in the Life Realm, to its *immortal soul* in the Soul Realm, to its *eternal idea* in the Mind Realm, and returns to its origin in The One. In this manner, the diviner pierces the veil of the subject-object dichotomy: by recognizing the divine intent shining through each symbol, one takes on the quality of the symbol, internalizes it, and ultimately shares in its meaning and intent.

Understanding the meaning of another manifestation, in other words, is not an external experience—it is one manifestation receiving the meaning of another manifestation, much as a mirror receives the image of an object and makes it its own in reflection. The diviner receives the meaning of a symbol, whereupon it exists in the diviner's awareness as the living embodiment of the *divine intent* with which it is imbued in the Act of Creation. Now, then, the identical meaning exists within the *symbol and the diviner*, both.

The essence of the diviner and the essence of the symbol are no longer two different things—this essence-to-essence communion embodies the act of *mystical union*, triggering the spontaneous ascension along the Axis Mundi and the diviner's reunion with The One.

Such *symbolic vision* is precisely the type of *mystical union* that collapses the subject-object duality and allows the diviner to step outside time and enter eternity.

While this is true for any symbol in Creation, it is even more so for the symbols of the divinatory method one uses, since they have a long history of acting as conduits of the Oracle's meaning. Whether it is the planet *Mercury* or the card *The Fool* or the trigram *Lake*, the symbols inherent to one's divinatory method provide a direct intuitive identification with the *Mind of the Oracle*.

Neither conceptual nor rational, the step outside time is a perceptible communion with the One Spirit and its all-at-once view of the timebound realm. These glimpses of the Oracle's omniscience further the diviner's surrender of individual will in order to be moved into action at the most opportune moment.

The magically right moment of *Kairos* ever occurs at the intersection of the *Crossroads of Creation*. It is from here that the *divine path* of each soul sets forth and to here that each returns.

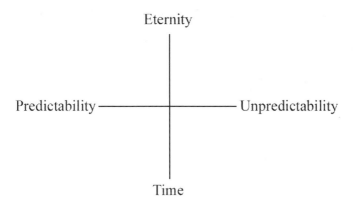

Diviners return to this center with each divination.

With each such return, the mysterious principle governing the *Kairos* of the converging *orders of Creation* reveals more of itself to the diviner's *symbolic vision*. Divine Intent reveals itself to be a *Sacred Game* of infinite variations in which every possible diversity of life and form is explored.

The two most important days of your life
Are the day you are born and the day you find out why.

~ Anonymous

The diviner's own *divine path* carries them into the heights of the transcendental realms and the depths of nature mysticism. They seldom originally intend to set foot on this path but coincidences and accidents and dreams somehow propel them into a regimen of sincere inquiry into the true nature of Creation. They nonetheless step onto a path of destiny, as it turns out, that makes of them an *inner void* wherein the union of Heaven and Earth might continue to produce offspring.

What leaps forth from the center point of *Kairos* is the sacred pyre of *Divine Fire* dancing the ecstatic vision of the infinite variations of every possible diversity of life and form. To *see* the omnipresent upwelling of Creation underlying the world of appearances is, for diviners across the ages, the awe-inspiring and humbling grace of being welcomed into the Mind of Heaven.

CONCLUSION

The greatest act of magic
is to be welcomed into the Mind of Heaven

There is perhaps no revelation quite as startling as finding out just how *personal* Creation is.

Those seeking to discover the true nature of the Mysteries of Creation do not enter into a lifetime of study and self-cultivation out of idle curiosity—rather, they dedicate themselves to this lifelong practice first, out of *devotion*, and then, out of *love*.

Devotion pours from the breast in spontaneous response to the grandeur of Creation. Love pours from the soul in spontaneous response to the Creative Spirit that bestows mortal life and cradles its immortality in mortal death.

It is the realization of the Creative Spirit's love for every being—and their sacrifices that fulfill the Divine Intent—

which triggers one's revelation. As the realization sets in that one is a unique eternal idea in the mind of the Creative Spirit, one comes to experience the Divine Love binding All Creation into its coherent Whole. It is the unique nature of each eternal idea that awakens the awareness of one's indelible place in the indivisible mind of the Creative Spirit.

Deathless and imperishable, one's true identity as an utterly unique eternal idea in the mind of the Creative Spirit dawns upon one's awareness slowly, over lifetimes, until the real clarity of understanding breaks through the fog of doubt and confusion: Divine Love is what gives birth to each of the eternal ideas, who, upon *remembering their origin*, return that love in measures beyond mortal reckoning.

To be welcomed into the Mind of Heaven, then, is to be *Welcomed Home*.

The art of divination and stepping outside time is a mystical practice and in no way mechanical. Like other mystical practices, such as alchemy, for example, it relies on a symbolic language to rekindle the individual's memory of their divine origin in the Act of Creation. It depends on the divine *Kairos* to awaken that memory at the appointed time.

Human beings live in the manifestation realm. Because every manifestation is a symbol, every human act is an act of interpretation. And, because every act of interpretation is an act of divination, every human being is a diviner.

What was said in the opening pages of this book bears repeating: while it aims to stand as a boon companion to all who *practice* divination, may it also serve as a worthy ally to all who *aspire* to the art.

SCHOOL OF RATIONAL MYSTICISM

DIVINATION:

> *The Toltec I Ching: 64 Keys to Inspired Action in the New World*
> with Martha Ramirez-Oropeza
> *In the Oneness of Time: The Education of a Diviner*
> *Way of the Diviner*

RESEARCHES ON THE TOLTEC I CHING:

> Vol. 1. *I Ching Mathematics: The Science of Change*
> Vol. 2. *The Image and Number Treatise*
> Vol. 3. *The Forest of Fire Pearls Oracle*
> Vol. 4. *I Ching Mathematics for the King Wen Version*
> Vol. 5. *Why Study the I Ching?*
> Vol. 6. *The Open Secret I Ching*
> Vol. 7. *The Alchemical I Ching*
> Vol. 8. *Intrachange: I Ching Chess*
> Vol. 9. *Before Heaven I Ching: Reading the Text of Creation*

SELF-REALIZATION PRACTICES:

> *The Five Emanations*
> *The Spiritual Basis of Good Fortune*
> *Facing Light*
> *The Soul of Power: Deconstructing the Art of War*
> *The Tao of Cool: Deconstructing the Tao Te Ching*
> *Fragments of Anamnesia*
> *We Are I Am: Visions of Mystical Union*

MISCELLANEOUS

POETRY:
> *Palimpsest Flesh*

NOVEL:
> *Life and Death in the Hotel Bardo*

Made in the USA
Middletown, DE
04 June 2021